Strategic Studies Institute
and
U.S. Army War College Press

A NEW TYPE OF GREAT POWER RELATIONSHIP BETWEEN THE UNITED STATES AND CHINA: THE MILITARY DIMENSION

Geoffrey Till

September 2014

*****

Comments pertaining to this report are invited and should be forwarded to: Director, Strategic Studies Institute and U.S. Army War College Press, U.S. Army War College, 47 Ashburn Drive, Carlisle, PA 17013-5010.

*****

This manuscript was funded by the U.S. Army War College External Research Associates Program. Information on this program is available on our website, *www.StrategicStudies Institute.army.mil*, at the Opportunities tab.

*****

*****

The Strategic Studies Institute and U.S. Army War College Press publishes a monthly email newsletter to update the national security community on the research of our analysts, recent and forthcoming publications, and upcoming conferences sponsored by the Institute. Each newsletter also provides a strategic commentary by one of our research analysts. If you are interested in receiving this newsletter, please subscribe on the SSI website at *www.StrategicStudiesInstitute.army.mil/newsletter*.

FOREWORD

For the United States and its allies and partners around the world, the debate about the pivot or rebalancing of American interests toward the Asia-Pacific Region is crucial. The United States has to ensure that allies and partners in other areas do not feel neglected or disadvantaged by the possible consequences of this initiative. To a large extent, this will depend not merely on how that initiative is presented, but also on the nature of the relationship between the United States and China. The more tense that relationship, and the more competitive rather than cooperative it is, the greater the likelihood of strategic distraction from other important areas of the world. China under President Xi Jinping is working out what it wishes that relationship to be, since it too recognizes that its nature will, in part, determine the peace and prosperity of the region. China also realizes that its nature will affect to a significant extent, the regime's capacity to ensure the continued economic development on which the Communist party's continued dominance depends.

For both countries, then, the stakes are high. President Xi has recently urged that China and the United States develop a new relationship between the two great powers. In this monograph, Dr Geoffrey Till explores what form that relationship may take, what its consequences are likely to be, and what options are available to the United States.

The manner in which the Armed Forces of the United States deployed into the Asia-Pacific are used to convey messages of reassurance and deterrence toward China will be a critical part of the package of necessary strategic policies toward the region. Although the region is overwhelmingly maritime in nature, the

U.S. Army has a number of essential roles to play in contributing toward this new relationship.

Douglas C. Lovelace

DOUGLAS C. LOVELACE, JR.
Director
Strategic Studies Institute and
   U.S. Army War College Press

ABOUT THE AUTHOR

GEOFFREY TILL, Dean of Academic Studies at the United Kingdom Command and Staff College from 1997-2006, is now Emeritus Professor of Maritime Studies at King's College London and Chairman of the Corbett Centre for Maritime Policy Studies. Since 2009, he has also been a Visiting Professor at the Rajaratnam School of International Studies, Singapore. He is also Adjunct Research Professor at the National Institute for the Study of the South China Sea, Haikou, Hainan, China. In addition to many articles and chapters on various aspects of maritime strategy and policy defense, Professor Till is the author of a number of books. His most recent is *Seapower: A Guide for the 21st Century, Third Ed.*, January 2013, for Routledge. He edited, with Patrick Bratton, *The Triumph of Neptune? Seapower and the Asia-Pacific: Adjusting to New Realities*; and an Adelphi Book for the International Institute for Strategic Studies, *Naval Expansion in Asia: An Arms Race in the Making?* Both were published by Routledge as paperbacks in 2013 and 2014. In 2013, with Jane Chan, he edited *Naval Modernisation in South-East Asia: Nature, Causes and Consequences*. His *Understanding Victory: Naval Operations from Trafalgar to the Falklands* is to be published by ABC-Clio in 2014. Professor Till is currently working on a number of other projects on maritime security in the Indo-Pacific region. His works have been translated into 12 languages.

SUMMARY

The relative rise of China is likely to lead a major shift in the world's strategic architecture, which the United States will need to accommodate. For the outcome to be generally beneficial, China needs to be dissuaded from hegemonic aspirations and retained as a cooperative partner in the world system. This will require a range of potentially conflicting thrusts in U.S. policy.

Since the Asia-Pacific Region is primarily a maritime theater, the U.S. Navy, Marines, and Air Force will need to play a leading role. The U.S. Army, nonetheless, will have a substantial supporting and facilitating role.

A NEW TYPE OF GREAT POWER RELATIONSHIP BETWEEN THE UNITED STATES AND CHINA: THE MILITARY DIMENSION

THE ISSUE

Power is the ability to influence through the strength of a country's armed forces, the wealth of its economy, or the hold it has over public opinion or the popular imagination.[1] Power is best understood as the relative capacity to influence the environment and human behavior. The instrumentalities of influence range across a spectrum from "soft power" (the socio-cultural dimension) through what some have called "sticky power" (the economic-industrial dimension) to "hard power" (the military-strategic dimension). Major shifts in relative power determined by dramatic changes in these three very closely related categories of influence have been a central characteristic of human history.

Nowadays the focus of attention is on a notional shift in relative power from "West" to "East." Contentions that "we are living through the end of 500 years of Western ascendancy"[2] and that Asia "is poised to increase its geopolitical and economic influence rapidly in the decades to come"[3] have become commonplace. To some, this is simply part of a historic pattern of continuous change and tectonic historic swings backward and forward from one to the other.[4] At the moment, the East is generally regarded as being in the ascendant, significantly rising relative to the West.[5]

Recently, this debate has narrowed from grand matters of the relative power of East and West, to the more specific issue of the future power relationship of China and the United States. This has led to vibrant

1

debate in China, the rest of the Asia-Pacific region, and in the United States about both the **extent** of the anticipated transformation in this bilateral strategic relationship and its projected **consequences**.[6]

The United States has announced its intention to resume paying the level of attention to the Asia-Pacific region that its strategic importance warrants. In President Barack Obama's words, "As a Pacific nation, the United States will play a larger and long-term role in shaping this region and its future, by upholding core principles and in close partnership with our allies and friends."[7]

In the wake of the American "rebalance" toward the Asia-Pacific, the requirement for the establishment of a new and positive strategic relationship between China and the United States seems the most fundamental of these consequences. Building such a relationship is key to the enduring national security objective of ensuring a safe, stable, and prosperous international environment.[8] This has been characterized by President Xi as "a new type of great power relationship" and by Washington as the "central, sort of, organizing principle" of international relations.[9] The chief characteristics of this new relationship—and the extent to which they will be shaped and illustrated by shifts in the soft, sticky, and hard aspects of relative national power and the implications of this for the role of the U.S. military in the region—demand closer consideration.

Soft Power: The Socio-cultural Dimension.

In the socio-cultural dimension, the Chinese language and Chinese concepts are clearly becoming more visible as the country's increasing wealth increases their geographic spread and depth. To some extent, this is a natural consequence of China's rise. But it is also the effect of deliberate state policy. The "Confucian Institutes," for example, which were established to win over public opinion in the outside world (something that historically was rarely of concern to the Chinese before the modern era) have proved successful. As many as 325 such institutes already exist around the world, and most have major development plans to be finalized before 2020.[10] The so-called "Pannikar tradition," in which, under the surface, most Asian countries resent the presence of outsiders in their region, provides a fruitful basis for the country's competitive "charm offensives" in Southeast Asia and elsewhere.[11] China's vision of a harmonized world based on traditional Chinese values has proved an effective, if not decisive, counter to what Beijing refers to as "the China threat theory" peddled by its adversaries.[12]

The perceived policy paralysis in Washington's ability to manage its economic difficulties and regional concerns about the reality of the U.S. pivot/rebalance toward Asia has at least temporarily decreased the credibility of the Western liberal narrative, while increasing the relative effectiveness of China's soft power. Some analysts in China urge the leadership to compete in the sphere of economic ideas by pushing the case for a Beijing consensus against the Western narrative of economic and social development based on liberal democracy.[13]

These analysts argue that opinion polls suggest major distinctions between the perceived trustworthiness of the U.S. Government and the attractions of "the American Dream," and that many are skeptical that the United States **will**, in fact, still be the leading power in 20 years. Even so, the U.S. image is still globally better than China's.[14] Nonetheless, norms about the freedom of the press, religion, and speech increasingly are being accepted as universal, not just Western ones, even in China itself. The United States seeks to take careful advantage of this.

Moreover, the fact that doubts about the rebalance are a matter of concern throughout Asia demonstrates the limits of China's soft power, especially when Beijing is perceived as being unduly assertive in its claims toward the South and East China Seas.[15] These limits, together with a memory of historic antagonisms (in the case, for example, of Vietnam and Japan) and local resentments about the sheer number and the personal styles of mainland Chinese flooding into Hong Kong, Singapore, and other parts of Southeast Asia as both tourists and temporary/permanent residents, reinforce the point. China's leadership must be aware of such limits to its soft power and of the potential liabilities that might accompany it.[16]

Further, a review of the shopping and eating places available in Shanghai and other such locations in China helps explain the widespread fear among those the West would call "hard-liners" about the extent to which Chinese governance styles and values are being subverted by Western cultural infiltration.[17] This fear, together with rising concern about the uneven effect of rapid industrialization on the domestic population, accounts for an almost certainly exaggerated fear in governmental and party circles about the survivability of the regime and its values.[18]

There are, then, obvious social and cultural tensions between the United States and China. A key question for American policymakers in framing their plan for strategic communications is how competitive this relationship is and should be, and how best to handle it. The healthy development of bilateral relations arguably will depend in significant measure on "soft" cultural exchanges.[19]

Sticky Power: The Economic-Industrial Dimension.

Few would deny the remarkable growth of China's gross domestic product (GDP) in recent years, which increased tenfold between 1978 and 2004, compared to fourfold for the United Kingdom (UK) between 1830 and 1900. As a result, China accumulated a current account surplus of 10 percent of GDP, while the United States, on the other hand, accounted for more than half the world's current account deficit at 6 percent of GDP.[20] A highly effective government stimulus program and massive credit expansion drawn from the world's biggest accumulated reserves—which is in turn derived from high levels of both savings and foreign investment—meant China recovered quickly from the crisis of 2007-09, with export levels 17 percent higher in 2009 than for 2008.[21] In 2000, the U.S. GDP was 8 times larger than China's; now it is only 4 times larger, and, according to Jim O'Neill, Goldman Sachs Chief economist, China's GDP will overtake that of the United States in 2027.[22] Many analysts, such as Professor Victor Sit of Hong Kong Baptist University, indeed argue that China's economic achievements to date should be seen essentially as providing the foundation for a Second Global Shift into a more sophisticated kind of economic prowess—characterized by high-tech engineering, the development of green energy, and a substantial move into the financial services.[23]

This appears to contrast strikingly with the general *angst*, for example, about American competitiveness and Washington's ability to handle systemic economic problems.[24] This development, if true (and there are plenty of reasons to doubt it[25]), would pose a substantial potential challenge—whether intended or not—to the future role of the U.S. dollar and to Washington's continued domination of the world economy. It is a new source of Chinese confidence and offers a major channel for China to shape its international context.[26] Reinforced by the obvious implications for defense spending, this development suggests that a significant shift in relative economic power is indeed under way, even if that may not amount to a future Chinese economy dominating the American.

But although the relative growth of Chinese economic power cannot be denied,[27] a number of points counterbalance this fact. First, as China industrializes, it creates problems for itself. These include weak local government finances and excessive amounts of domestic debt, inadequate banking system loans, the future costs of an aging population, a probable debt-to-GDP ratio of 65 percent,[28] and a low governmental tax-take relative to the GDP. As incomes rise, China will lose the competitive advantage of low-cost labor and increase the dangers of a middle-income trap. To this must be added the often relegated social tensions remarked on earlier.[29] The regime can only hope to resolve these pressures by the domestic investment of a goodly proportion of its newfound sources of wealth. Nor, according to former premier Wen Jiabao can there be total confidence that such problems **are** soluble in the near future.[30] These pressures, he argued, mean that currently the Chinese economy is "unstable, unbalanced, uncoordinated, and unsustainable" and that accordingly it would be "foolish to postulate that the 21st century will belong to China."[31] Wen Jiabao is but one of many Chinese implicitly pointing out the unwisdom of confusing the **size** of an economy with its **strength**. The 2012 *Chinese Defense White Paper* indeed makes the point that the U.S. economic recovery will make it harder for China to catch up with the United States.

This raises a number of important issues. Setting relative indicators of raw elements of the economic performance of China and the United States against each other is misleading in two ways. First, the strength of an economy has to be set not just against that of other countries, but also against the challenge of its own commitments. Second, it is by no means clear that any relative rise in China's economic strength, when set against that of the United States — and which may emerge even from this more sophisticated measure of comparison — is necessarily against American interests. Many would argue the precise reverse, in fact. In 1971, bilateral trade between the two countries came to less than $5 million; the United States now does more trade with China in a single hour.[32]

Such is the level of mutually beneficial economic interdependence between the two countries that a major failure in China could have catastrophic effects on the global economy, and therefore on the United States itself. Indeed, some worry that the internal social and economic pressures listed above will require Beijing to give greater priority to its domestic market and may make the economy rather more autarchic than it is now. In turn, this could lower the level of economic interdependence, making it significantly less of a bonding mechanism between the two countries. What, in fact, emerges from this review of the economic dimension of China's relative rise is that, despite the astounding nature of China's recent economic performance, its future trajectory and possible consequences remain uncertain and ambiguous, and may depend in large measure on U.S. policy and the fortunes of the U.S. economy. What also emerges, however, are the potential tensions between American and Chinese conceptions of the global economic system and how it should develop.[33]

Hard Power: The Military Dimension.

Since the health of the economy is fundamental to defense spending, the narrative of the decline of the United States relative to China is almost as strong in the military power dimension as it is in the industrial-economic one. There are major systemic differences in the defense spending of the two countries (such as cheaper labor costs in China but more social defense spending). This, plus the relative lack of transparency in Chinese budgeting, makes it difficult to compare the two budgets. But even according to official figures, Chinese defense spending is increasing, and, by 2025, could easily reach half the American level.[34]

Again, such raw comparisons based on bean counting (whether those beans are billions of dollars, or naval platforms and systems) are inadequate in themselves. Calculations of relative military **strength** as measured by the capacity to decide outcomes have to include the degree of challenge posed to a country by the scale and nature of its perceived commitments. In this more nuanced mode of assessment, the U.S. Navy, for example, is challenged by the sheer diversity of the scenarios for which it feels it has to prepare. This is true whether it's a question of having to prepare a wide variety of mission capabilities, both to cope with asymmetric techno-tactical anti-access strategies ranging from terrorists on jet skis to the anti-ship ballistic missile strategies of the Chinese and the very different conditions pertaining to the Western Pacific, the Indian Ocean, the Gulf and Red Sea, the Gulf of Aden, the Mediterranean, the Caribbean, and, to some extent, the Atlantic theaters of operation.[35] These considerations dissipate the U.S. Navy and make it more difficult for it to assemble that concentration of force that Mahan advocated so strongly. Further, "[f]or the first time since 1890 . . . the U.S. Navy is faced with the prospect of competing against a potentially hostile naval power possessing a ship-building capacity that is equal to if not superior, to its own"[36] — in some respects at least.

That is the reason for the concerns in Washington about trends in the correlation of naval, and, indeed, air forces, in the Western Pacific and the possibility that the U.S. military may be on the verge of significant decline relative to China. These concerns were exacerbated by the administration's sequestration difficulties. Thus, the Chief of Naval Operations, Admiral Jonathan Greenert, stated: "We'll have inadequate surge capacity at the appropriate readiness to be there when it matters. . . . We will not be able to respond in the way the nation has expected and depended (on us to act)." In an open letter to Congress, 45 prominent analysts concluded that such short- and long-term difficulties ". . . will degrade our ability to defend our allies, deter aggression, and promote American economic interests. . . . It will erode the credibility of our treaty commitments abroad."[37]

By contrast, China is seen as engaging in a major modernization of its land and air forces and, most significantly, given the maritime nature of the Asia-Pacific region, in a potentially transformational rise in the level of its naval aspirations. The development of China's naval nuclear power, for example, seems likely to boost China's foreign policy confidence. Thus, a *Global Times* editorial in October 2013 stated:

> China is powerful in possessing a credible second-strike nuclear capability. . . . Some countries haven't taken this into serious consideration when constituting their China policy, leading to a frivolous attitude towards China in public opinion account. . . . China needs to make it clear that the only choice is not to challenge China's core interest. . . . Developing marine-based nuclear power is part of such work.[38]

Building up the navy is a critical part of China's long-stated intention to develop as a maritime power. On July 11, 2005, China inaugurated its first Navigation Day to commemorate Admiral Zheng He's first voyage in the 15th century. Seven years later, in his last speech at the "Big 18" National Party Congress in 2012, President Hu Jintao argued for, ". . . enhancing the Chinese capacity for exploiting marine resources, resolutely safeguarding China's maritime rights and interests, and building China into a maritime power."[39]

This message was strongly reinforced by the first major speech of his successor, President Xi, on the subject, which, significantly, took place on the guided missile destroyer *Haikou*.[40] China's urge to the sea, moreover, is robustly maritime, not just naval. The stress of energy and also food security means it incorporates far more than just shipping, ship-building, and associated industries. China's growing interest in the Arctic demonstrates that it is global in scope. Practical progress and the extent of China's institutional reform (for example, its coast guard agencies) shows how seriously these maritime aspirations are taken.[41]

Given the traditional land-centric and continental focus of Chinese strategic culture,[42] this latter development has struck many observers as particularly worrying. China is developing more ambitious naval forces, and even more significantly, the maritime industries that historically tend to go with them.[43] Almost equally inevitably, these will challenge the U.S. strategic primacy in the Western Pacific, a geographic area of strategic maneuver hitherto dominated by American naval/air power. Given its many other global commitments and the likely impact of reduced levels of defense spending in the years ahead, the U.S. Navy is particularly sensitive to these developments. This sensitivity is reflected in the "rebalance" toward the Asia-Pacific, the "Air-Sea Battle construct," and the current U.S. naval preoccupation with political, technological, and operational ways of maintaining required levels of access to the waters of the Western Pacific in these new and more challenging circumstances.[44]

Such perceptions may need, however, to be caveated. First, it is easy to exaggerate the **extent** of China's naval rise, its first carrier and growing amphibious capability notwithstanding. Most estimates suggest that for all its current difficulties, the U.S. military in general, and its naval and air forces in particular, will remain far more capable than the Chinese at least for the next couple of decades.[45] Second, it is possible to interpret China's greatly increased level of investment in the People's Liberation Army Navy (PLAN) as an unremarkable illustration of a historically natural and now economically sustainable response of a country with developing maritime interests both in its near seas and more distantly, to enhance its capacity to defend those interests. Offshore, China has substantial economic and strategic interests most obviously in the South and East China Seas, an area from which, in the recent past, its national security has been threatened.

China's growing presence on the world ocean, such as its participation in the international counterpiracy mission off Somalia and the presence of an air-defense frigate standing off the coast of Libya, while thousands of its citizens were evacuated from the perils of a local civil war, reflect the country's integration with the global trading system—a process that inevitably expands China's international interests and security obligations. The first of these, at least, called for cooperation with the U.S. Navy rather than competition, still less confrontation.

Once again, the extent of China's relative military rise and the motivation and consequences of that rise remain a legitimate area for debate. These are likely to be quite significantly affected, among other things, by American policy.

Alternative Futures.

A shift, then, is taking place across all three dimensions of power—soft, sticky, and hard. It is evidenced not just by greater economic and military strength, but by China's greater diplomatic weight at the United Nations (UN), as illustrated by its role in the management of the North Korean problem and its influence in the ongoing debate over Libya, Syria, and Iran. Some anticipate radical change in the global economic system, expecting a set of governing and operating principles more collective, less individual, more state-centric, less liberal. In other words, the Yuan will replace the dollar, and Mandarin will take over from English—Globalization with Chinese characteristics.[46] The immediate consequences were made clear by Ruan Zongze in the *Peoples' Daily*:

Today, China, because of its rapidly rising strength, sits at the main table on the global stage, and needs to get used to newly being in the limelight. The international community also needs to adjust to China's new role.[47]

Hence the key question, if the *status quo* is not defensible and some degree of strategic change seems inevitable, which of the possible alternative futures in system change, both in terms of outcomes and the means by which those outcomes are delivered, would seem the most beneficial—or the least harmful—to U.S. interests? There are clearly a variety of such outcomes, with varying degrees of acceptability to Washington.

A Zero-Sum Shift.

History suggests, unfortunately, that war and conflict often accompany systemic change, as the incumbent great power either defeats a challenger or succumbs to it.[48] As Niall Ferguson succinctly comments, "Major shifts in the balance of power are seldom amicable." In China, as elsewhere, there are hawks who most definitely think along such potentially confrontational lines.[49] There cannot be, they say, "two tigers on one mountain." It would also be as well to remember that with its combination of economic power and hard military power, China is potentially the most formidable challenge the United States has ever come across, especially when it might turn itself into a major nuclear weapons state. Previous outcomes to such confrontations (which would include World Wars I and II, and the Cold War) underline the wisdom of Henry Kissinger's observation that:

Neither [the US and China] has much practice in co-operative relations with equals. Yet their leaders have no more important task than to implement the truths that neither country will ever be able to dominate the other, and that conflict between them would exhaust their societies and undermine the prospects of world peace.[50]

Heightened Rivalry and Increased Multipolarity.

A second somewhat less immediately apocalyptic possibility would be of continued U.S.-China rivalry against a background of increased multipolarity with high levels of state versus state competition, reminiscent perhaps of Europe before World War I, and as characterized perhaps by the tensions between Japan and China over the islands of the East China Sea, or, in a somewhat lesser key, between Japan and South Korea.[51] Most analysts would reject this as a desired outcome, first because of what the European example led to, and, second, because of a systemically greater need for a collective global response to common threats like international crime, environmental degradation, international terrorism, economic recessions and depressions, and so forth.

Lowered Rivalry and Increased Multipolarity.

Recognition of this need may, instead, lead to a third kind of outcome — greater multipolarity but with less state-on-state competition, in which the key interests of all major stakeholders are sufficiently accommodated. Since China appears to be "catching up" with the United States faster than other countries such as India or Russia are catching up with China, the resultant multipolarity would seem likely to have a distinctly bipolar edge to it, though it would be in the interest of neither great power to seek to develop this relationship in "G2" terms.

Nonetheless, such an outcome anticipates the United States and China acting to a significant extent as security partners in a wider, more multipolar, world. In such a world, the individual and distinctive agendas of a host of other countries in a notably diverse region act as both a restraint and — possibly playing one off against the other — an encouragement to both of the main actors in the drama, as has been done before elsewhere. This will ensure that neither emerges as the sole superpower.[52] This is plainly what Singapore among other U.S. partners would wish to see:

> The rise of China does not imply the decline of the United States. And we in Singapore do not subscribe to the declinist theory . . . the world and Asia are big enough to accommodate both a rising China and a reinvigorated US.[53]

All the same, a distinctly competitive edge to the relationship between the United States and China in this construct seems likely to remain. Hence, in this relationship, an element of mutual deterrence would need to co-exist along with the reassurance in U.S. policy. Nonetheless, this kind of calibrated and defensive balancing would, in effect, be much less provocative than outright competition.[54]

Peaceful Replacement.

The final alternative outcome is of one major power stepping down and being replaced by another peacefully, as illustrated by the supplanting of Britain as the world's leading power in the 19th century by the United States in the 20th. As a process, this is in some ways the most benign of all outcomes. But it was not without its own tensions and difficulties[55] and is in any case unlikely to be accepted by a United States, which doubts its necessity or may be reluctant to entrust its core national interests to the protection of another state, or group of states, especially one with significantly different values.

Accordingly, of these four alternative outcomes, some variant of the third option, namely, greater multipolarity but with less state-on-state competition, would seem to have the greatest appeal. This requires the retention within a broadly cooperative rules-based international system of China as a major military and trading power, with national interests to defend and incentives to work substantially with others against common threats. There is, however, likely to be some robust debate about what those rules are.[56] The Chinese never cease to point out that institutions like the World Bank, the Organization for Economic Cooperation and Development, and the International Money Fund are dominated by the West and need to change rather more than they are changing. The key issue here would seem to be the extent to which China seeks to make new rules — or whether the old ones will make China.

Nonetheless, engaging positively with China was one of the major publicly stated motivations for the rebalance toward the Asia-Pacific:

> A key objective of our rebalance is to build a healthy, transparent and sustainable U.S.-China defense relationship, one that supports a broader relationship . . . a strong and cooperative U.S.-China partnership is essential for global security and prosperity in the 21st Century.[57]

The United States, in effect, will need to accommodate China's views more than it used to and prompt a reconsideration of the rebalance toward the Asia-Pacific. For China's part, President Xi has made his view of the four required principles, in what he calls a "new type of great power relationship," fairly clear. Both sides should:

1. Use existing intergovernmental mechanisms for communication and dialogue;

2. Utilize trade and exchanges on technology to open new channels of cooperation;

3. Coordinate their policies on major international issues; and,

4. Develop a new pattern of military relations.[58]

Nonetheless, the extent and consequence of this strategic shift and the new relationship between Beijing and Washington remains ambiguous. One of the reasons is that this shift, at least to a large extent, is contingent on the direction and success of U.S. policy.

OUTLINES OF A RESPONSE

Denying Denial.

Sufficient changes are afoot to suggest that a substantial reappraisal of U.S. policy toward China as an emerging great power is called for, even if the extent and consequence of that rise as yet remain ambiguous, and may mean no more than a shrinking ratio of American superiority. Hence, the value of Hugh White's warning against what he calls the four common denials about China's future is to be found among those who do not accept the need for the reappraisal of the necessity for some form of accommodation between Beijing and Washington, namely,

1. China is not really growing economically that much;

2. China will not attain sufficient strategic weight;

3. China will not choose to use its strategic weight, as to do so is not in its interest; and,

4. Even if China does so choose, it will necessarily lose.[59]

On this basis, there would not be much need for the United States to re-evaluate substantially its current course of policy.

The declinist debate about the **extent** to which the United States will have to cede at least elements of its supremacy to China remains unresolved, but, for all that, there is little doubt that something of a strategic shift is indeed taking place.[60] As Ambassador Charles W. Freeman, Jr. has observed:

> In some disturbing ways, Sino-American competition is beginning to parallel the contest between us and the Soviet Union in the Cold War. This time, however, the United States is in the fiscally precarious position of the USSR, while China plays the economically robust role we once did.[61]

That may be an exaggeration of the robustness of the Chinese economy and an underestimation of U.S. resilience, but, even so, none of these four denials serve as a reliable basis for sensible policymaking. "Americans will need to move beyond the myth," Christopher Layne concludes, "that the United States is somehow immune from the forces of change that history has unleashed."[62] Exaggerated notions of what the "No. One Power" represents and can, in any case, achieve may also need restraint.

Outlines of a Policy.

Evidently, there is a need for a clear-sighted and pragmatic policy of retaining China as a major stakeholder in a more multipolar world system and a prospective security and economic partner of the United States. This stands midway between the panda-hugging and dragon-slaying extremes of recommended American policy. It differs radically from the containment options of "Mr. X" when confronting the Soviet Union of the late-1940s, in that there is no thought of the holding back of a major and essentially malignant new power until its internal contradictions change it into a more benign one. Any attempt to contain China sequentially in this way is likely to be counterproductive, not the least because a policy would be most unwelcome in much of Asia. Instead, the emphasis is on the **simultaneous** transmission of messages of reassurance and deterrence, both intended to convey that China's rise is to be welcomed as a responsible security partner. Putting it simply, the aim would be to provide incentives for "good" behavior and disincentives for "bad" — and in both cases to range across the whole of the soft-sticky-hard dimensions of power. Critically, the aim needs also to involve wider engagement with other players in a more multipolar world.

There are three dimensions to such a policy:
- Deterrence — providing disincentives to unwelcome behavior;
- Reassurance — providing incentives to welcome behavior; and,
- Wider Engagement with other players in an increasingly multilateral setting in order to support U.S. policies of deterrence and reassurance as necessary.

There are good reasons for caution about this policy, and two initial points need to be made immediately. First, the U.S. capacity to engage in a nuanced and effective program of deterrence and reassurance is itself much more conditional than often appears to be the case. The extent to which China's trajectory **can** be shaped easily by American policy initiatives may be exaggerated. To a large extent, China has always marched to the sound of its own drums. This is true in terms both of domestic political and institutional constraints and of traditional cultural values — refined and consolidated by 5,000 years of history. As Kissinger has warned, these distinctive values and their possible effects need to be understood. For example:

> A principal difference between Chinese and western diplomatic strategy is the reaction to perceived vulnerability. American and western diplomats conclude that they should move carefully to avoid provocation; the Chinese response is more likely to magnify defiance.[63]

That said, "a calibrated combination of rewards and punishments, and majestic cultural performance" were arguably what preserved China through thousands of years of turbulence. Logically, the country's leaders may well understand, and even prove surprisingly receptive to, such a policy, even one emanating from Washington.[64] Nonetheless, there is a need for some becoming modesty in Washington's appraisal of what it can and should do to mold Chinese perceptions.

Moreover, its relationship with the United States is far from being the sole, or even necessarily the main, preoccupation of a Chinese leadership concerned above all with providing the kind of internal social

20

and economic development that ultimately will be the main way of ensuring the survival of the current regime. For this reason, China is independently engaging in its own pivot toward Central Asia, Africa, South America, and the Middle East—not necessarily in some grand game of global rivalry with the United States, but mainly because its requirement for resources and markets demands it.[65]

This feeds into the second assumption that needs to be made about China's being a responsible security partner, namely, that there is a sufficient constituency of support for the notion of sharing power within China itself. Some Developmentalists would argue the unwisdom of China's assuming the burdens of even an informal empire. Instead, they argue, Beijing should focus on more limited aims, simply to win the status needed to help create conditions in East Asia conducive to the country's economic development and the continued stability of the regime as it proceeds through its program of calibrated reform.[66] China is represented as a still-developing country, and its involvement in the system should be designed to meet those internal needs.

There are a number of difficulties here, however. China frequently has exhibited a marked reluctance to assume the burdens of being a responsible stakeholder, preferring instead to devote those resources to its immediate internal needs. This might explain, perhaps, China's limited and tardy response to the Haiyun typhoon disaster in the Philippines.[67]

Other Chinese skeptics concerning the notion of the country's acting as a responsible stakeholder, on the other hand, argue that China's intention should be to seek an East Asia that resembles the ancient past—Sino-centric, hierarchical, deferential, but reasonably stable—and that a substantial U.S. role in the area would be unnecessary and unwelcome.[68] These are complex issues much debated by scholars.

Among other points they make is that in its 5,000 years of history, China has actually played different roles in East Asia, from victim to suzerain, from promoting the policies of openness and mutual respect characteristic of the Tang dynasty to the greater levels of control manifested by the Yuan and Ming dynasties.[69] The "All Under Heaven" *Tianxia* system, in which China is at the center of a deferential universe of smaller-state vassals benignly looked after while the barbarians are kept at arm's length, goes deep in the Chinese psyche. It presupposes China setting the rules of such a harmonious world.[70] Skepticism about the adoption of the role defined by the United States as a responsible stakeholder is further reinforced by the sense that the rules of the current game historically have been set by Washington and its allies, with little Chinese involvement.

A third group, the Internationalist Globalists, argue, on the contrary, that in its own economic and strategic interests, a rising China needs to integrate itself into the world economic system and help shape its future as a responsible stakeholder. Thus *Liaowang*, a leading party foreign affairs journal, says, in a much-cited article:

> Compared with past practices, China's diplomacy has indeed displayed a new face. If China's diplomacy before the 1980s stressed safeguarding of national security, and its emphasis from the 1980s to early this century is on the creation of an excellent environment for economic development, then the focus at present is to take a more active part in international affairs and play the role that a responsible power should on

the basis of satisfying the security and development interests.[71]

It is difficult to gauge the relative strength of these three grouped responses or their future trajectories, but they do represent a variety of shades of opinion. The entrepreneurial middle class will tend to favor the third option; the military and representatives of the still massive state-owned enterprises, the second. The United States therefore has to work on the various potentially conflicting schools of thought within the country.[72] Assuming and acting as though the hegemonists within China **are** the dominant group[73] is likely to prove a self-fulfilling prophecy for the United States. The problem is compounded by the fact that as yet, there is no longer a leading Mao-like figure predominant in setting China's security agenda; instead, there is a shoal of conflicting agencies and views ranging from the hard to the soft liners. Nonetheless, President Xi seems already to have won for himself a level of state authority not enjoyed by his two predecessors. His immediate assumption of the chair of the Central Military Commission and creation of a nascent National Security Council emphasize the point. President Xi's own take on the issue is therefore likely to be key to future developments, even if he is operating within a more pluralistic and constraining context than is often assumed. That being so, his earlier U.S. residence (and, indeed, the fact that his daughter is studying at Harvard) may suggest an encouraging degree of open-mindedness on the issue of China's developing relationship with the United States.[74]

Messages of Deterrence.

That said, the Chinese military remains an important constituency, which on the whole tends to be more hawkish than many party officials in the Ministry of Foreign Affairs, or Commerce. This hawkishness is tempered, however, by the military's strategic-cultural emphasis on the notions of active defense and its professional prudence and awareness of the military realities. Accordingly, there is scope for the exertion of a degree of deterrent pressure on Chinese assertiveness, should this be seen to recur. All the same, Beijing exhibits a marked propensity to push back when under pressure or challenged, a characteristic much illustrated by its policy in the disputed South and East China Seas.

In addition to this the extent of the public reaction to such events as the bombing of the Chinese Embassy in Belgrade, the air collision between Chinese and American aircraft near Hainan in 2001, and rising tensions in the South and East China Seas demonstrates the existence of a growing nationalist sentiment within China (and, indeed, elsewhere in the Western Pacific). This sentiment, when empowered by the tools of the social media, can hardly be ignored by any government, whatever its political hue or means of containing it.

Moreover, as remarked earlier, the policy effect of such groups may be reinforced by the existence of a strategic culture that features, for example, what Kissinger calls "offensive deterrence." This involves ". . . the use of a pre-emptive strategy not so much to defeat the adversary as to deal him a psychological blow to cause him to desist." To an extent, such reactions to external events are the default setting.[75]

Some Chinese policy initiatives do, indeed, seem to emanate from hard-line circles, not the least the extent to which the regime is implicated in the widespread cyberattacks on the United States and other sites. Such initiatives clearly demand a robust response.[76] A pragmatic acceptance of the existence of hard-line opinion-formers in China and the unwelcome policy initiatives that they may produce consequently means that a realistic policy has to include the provision, when necessary, of disincentives for unhelpful behavior and policies. Such a policy therefore demands a degree of deterrence.

The United States, as the world's biggest economy, leading military power, and a major source of global values, is in a good position to engage in policies of calibrated deterrence when there is a need. The extent of its military decline vis-à-vis China, and indeed everyone else, should not be exaggerated. The United States spends more than eight times on defense than does China. Moreover, of the top nine defense spenders, four are allies — the UK, France, Japan, and Germany and one a partner, Saudi Arabia. U.S. spending comfortably exceeds the rest of the nine put together — $739 billion to $486 billion.[77] If partners such as South Korea and Singapore are factored in as well, the total goes higher still. U.S. defense spending is still only some 4.4 percent of its GDP, more than most countries, but less than some and is, in strictly economic terms,[78] easily affordable. Certainly, even now the United States is nowhere near the level of defense spending that contributed to the fall of the Soviet Union. China's level of defense spending by comparison is notoriously hard to measure, but almost any calculation suggests that, although China is catching up, there remains a huge gap in military spending between the two countries.[79]

As a result, in the Pacific, it will be many years before Washington's commanding lead in deployable air and naval power is seriously compromised:

> The consensus of sources is that the size and level of operational experience of the U.S. Navy and Air Force makes it nearly impossible for potential opponents to mount a serious challenge in the waters and air space over the world's oceans. This is likely to continue until 2035.[80]

The obvious exception to this, though, may be the much narrower waters of the Western Pacific, where the gap between the two countries could prove considerably less.

More widely, Washington's deterrent capability is sustained by the continuing appeal of the U.S. dream; and for all the country's current budgetary problems, that dream remains strong, and its economy is still regarded as the essential motor of the world economy. The U.S. image—its capacity to win and influence friends in the Asia-Pacific and to avoid playing into the hands of the Chinese hegemonic constituency, however—depends on avoiding the appearance that the United States is "looking for a fight." For this reason, deterrence needs to be recessed, pragmatic, nonconfrontational, and, hence, frequently silent, so far as the media and much of the outside world is concerned—over such matters as the Chinese declaration of a new Air Defense Zone in the East China Sea. But private persuasion behind closed doors is likely to be more effective than repeated and ostentatious displays of American resolve.[81]

Accordingly, using these power advantages in order to make disincentives for bad behavior clear has to be carefully calibrated—first, that such use is seen by Beijing as credible; second, that it does not feed the paranoia of the hard-liners and encourage their rise relative to that of the soft-liners inside China's policymaking circles; third, that it does not trigger the instinctive rather than thinking cultural reactions described by Kissinger; and, fourth, that it does not unduly upset the other Asian powers. As a general rule, the further up the soft power/hard power scale they are, the more likely responses are to have these negative effects. Even so, they may be necessary in some cases.

China is well aware of the dangers of encirclement, but may need to be shown that in its assertive behavior in the East, and especially the South China Seas, it is in danger of encircling itself. Hence, likely local reactions to assertive acts may also act as a deterrent to such acts.[82]

Messages of Reassurance.

But alongside acting as a deterrent, the successful retention of China as a security partner will require the United States to provide ample reassurance that its intentions toward China are not malign, and that it welcomes, in fact as well as in rhetoric, the country's resumption of its proper place in the world order. This policy rests, of course, on the assumption that China is willing to share responsible power with the United States, as Beijing says, and is not secretly aiming at predominance either within the region or globally. There is room for doubt about this, as Kurt Campbell in one of his last interviews as Assistant Secretary of State pointed out:

> . . . We have done everything possible to encourage China to play a leading role in the G20, in the East Asia

Summit, just every imaginable institution and venue. But in many respects, China is ambivalent about playing that role.[83]

Because of the various constituencies of opinion about such reassurances, Beijing may need to be persuaded into being a responsible Great Power and accepting the political and economic costs that go with it. One paradoxical characteristic of this role is the occasional need to accept being bullied by the weak and to moderate, or even withdraw, policies that prove deeply unwelcome to the irritatingly presumptuous smaller fry clustered around one's heels. Persuasion accordingly requires the provision of positive incentives for good behavior.

What is encouraging, as discussed earlier, is the wealth of evidence suggesting that the advantages of a cooperative relationship with the United States is widely recognized within Chinese policymaking circles. If the economic development of China, the solution of its many domestic problems, and, indeed, the survival of the regime are China's top priorities, then a fruitful economic relationship with the world's largest and generally most successful economy is recognized as essential. Unsurprisingly, then, trade between the two countries is steadily rising. Worth approximately $100 billion in 2003, it doubled to $200 billion in 2005, rose to $300 billion in 2007, to $406 billion in 2011, and in 2012, topped $500 billion.

The consequent need for mutual understanding is evidenced by the existence of more than 60 mechanisms for official U.S.-China discussions. Presidents Hu and Obama met 13 times, and at Sunnylands in Rancho Mirage, CA, Obama and Xi appear to have gotten off to a good start.[84] Such contacts are reinforced by a plethora of more informal ones, such as the two-way tourist trade, huge numbers of student exchanges, and so forth. Although the notion of Chimerica can be pushed too far, there is certainly evidence of mutual dependence in the economic relations between the two countries, even perhaps a degree of convergence.[85]

This reflects, and indeed strengthens, the existence of soft-liners in China, who wish China to adopt a responsible stakeholder position alongside the United States, and who are well aware of the dangers of drifting into strategic rivalry. The notion of China's soft power has been widely discussed in China[86] — (hence the push for Confucian Institutes), and Beijing is perfectly aware that perceived assertiveness in the East and South China Seas has made its neighbors more wary.

Moreover, there is a great deal of diversity even among the soft-liners about what China should do in practical terms to secure this new relationship with the United States, differences that reflect a greater variety of opinion about how China should develop in general. Nor is there any doubt about the fact that there are limitations to the concessions China can make in order to be seen as a responsible stakeholder. Thus, in his first Presidential address, Xi was noticeably tougher than his predecessors in making this point clear:

> [N]o country should presume that we will engage in trade involving our core interests or that we will swallow the bitter fruit of harming our sovereignty, security, or development interests. . . . [China would] . . . stick to the road of peaceful development but never give up our legitimate rights and never sacrifice our national core interests.[87]

In his foreign policy initiatives, Xi has to balance between contending domestic forces, as does everyone else. China has real concerns about U.S. policy, which need to be, and indeed are being, addressed.[88]

Therefore, the United States has to present and explain its policies carefully. Many would see Obama's pivot/rebalance toward Asia as a prime example of how **not** to present policy. Arguably, its first appearance fed paranoia in Beijing that the policy was essentially a military *demarche* toward China (and so sustained the hard-liners). Then, when its real limits became clear, the policy troubled them further by revealing the limits of American power at a time of sequestration. The policy alienated other countries in Asia, who concluded that it looked like the policy of containing China in which they did not wish to participate. The policy also mystified local U.S. partners, who felt insufficiently consulted and were not sure of their role in it. The assumed association of the rebalance with the much misunderstood Air-Sea Battle construct reinforced misperceptions of both. Furthermore, U.S. allies and partners in other areas became concerned that their interests would be neglected. The fact that much of the rebalance was a perfectly natural response to the running-down of the Iraq and Afghanistan commitments and hence a return to normal, and that the military dimension was a relatively small aspect of the rebalance, got lost in the noise. Arguably, it would have been better not to have announced the initiative with such fanfare, but simply, quietly, to have gotten on with it. In crafting a new security relationship with China, such "bumper-sticker" strategies are more hindrance than help in a policy designed to assuage, not exploit, China's anxieties, while protecting U.S. interests in the region.[89]

Given the reluctance of most Asian states to take sides in a great power rivalry between China and the United States, and the need to secure a sustainable balance of interests between them, the United States has to engage in a policy of careful conciliation alongside its deterrence of Chinese assertiveness.[90]

Wider Engagement.

The third and final constituent of a policy of helping to turn China into a security partner is, at the same time, seeking the support of other partners in a more multipolar world. In such a world, there will be other significant rising players, both in the region (Japan, Korea, Australia, the Association of Southeast Asian Nations [ASEAN], and Indonesia) and, outside the region; these countries include India, Brazil, Mexico, South Africa, the European Union [EU], Saudi Arabia, and Russia. Responsibility for the direction of the world's affairs will be rather more shared than it used to be. Russia and China tend to call this the "democratization of international relations,"[91] and are clearly anxious to facilitate such a process.

This can be a helpful process for the United States in two ways. First, all these countries, to a greater or lesser extent, face the same range of problems— the dangers of recession and depression, organized transnational crime, mass migration, global warming, pandemics, and international terrorism, which can only be addressed by serious collective action and effective global or at least regional governance. They have a significant share in the global economy and, in consequence, an interest in advancing solutions to global challenges.

Second, most countries in the region do not want to answer, or even to be asked, "Whose side are you on?" in any strategic competition between the United States and China. Their differing levels of economic dependence on China is one of the main reasons, but their attitude may also suggest implicit assumptions about the strategic unwisdom of facilitating the emergence of "China versus the Rest" structures in the Asia-Pacific region, which would take it back to unwanted and potentially dangerous forms of bilateralism. For this reason, the United States needs to tread a careful line between encouraging closer relations among the countries of the region and seeming to seek to marshal these countries into an anti-Beijing coalition. Nonetheless, a number of them, especially in the Indo-Pacific region, have their own reservations about aspects of China's possible future trajectory and may seek comfort in each other's company.[92] Beijing is perfectly well aware of this fact and of the damage that overassertive behavior in the South and East China Seas can do to its charm offensives by reinforcing, rather than undermining, the China threat theory. This acts as a systemic constraint on aggressively nationalistic policies.

These two points strengthen the notion that constructively engaging with other countries, perhaps especially in the Western Pacific, will play a key role in a general policy of encouraging China to become a U.S. partner and perhaps an even more significant security provider in the global system. No other country seems as well placed as the United States to engage in this kind of focused consensus-building leadership.[93]

The importance of a considered and energetic engagement with the rest of the countries of the Western Pacific is reinforced by the fact that one consequence of China's rise is that it puts some of Washington's local alliances under great strain. In such maritime disputes as those over the islands of the South and East China Seas, the United States has to steer a complex course between providing sufficient support to allies and partners like Japan and the Philippines, while not enough to encourage entangling adventurism. As such recent events over the Scarborough and Second Thomas shoals in 2012-13, and over China's declaration of an air defense identification zone (ADIZ) in December 2013, have shown, this can be a tricky line to follow.

In spite of that, the other countries of East Asia, sensitively engaged, have a substantial contribution to make to the mixed deterrence/reassurance policies that could help China become a true security partner for the United States, rather than a hegemonic threat. Heightened awareness in Beijing of the reactions and importance of local states should act as a significant incentive for truly harmonious policies.

IMPLICATIONS FOR THE U.S. MILITARY

Introduction.

In order to facilitate China's rise as a responsible stakeholder, the United States will need to develop initiatives designed to deter, reassure, and garner the support of other states. Although the U.S. military in the Asia-Pacific has a key contribution to make to such a policy, there is a good deal more to such an exercise than that. Political, economic, and social initiatives, in many cases, will be far more important. But as Hillary Clinton nonetheless has remarked, the military role is indispensible if the full spectrum of possible events is to be adequately covered:

The U.S. will be better positioned to support humanitarian missions; equally important, working with more allies and partners will provide a more robust bulwark against threats or efforts to undermine regional peace and security.[94]

The Asia-Pacific is generally recognized as a primarily maritime region. Great sections of the world's largest ocean lie between most of its leading actors. The region's economy depends absolutely on sea traffic and, to an increasing extent, on fish and energy resources to be found at sea. In consequence, many countries in the region are rapidly developing the maritime elements of their economies, including China. There are numerous challenges to that sea dependence. Among them is the great skein of island and jurisdictional disputes stretching from the north of Japan to the Bay of Bengal. Not surprisingly, a substantial buildup of naval/air forces is taking place around the region. Not unnaturally, then, the U.S. Navy, Marines, and Air Force are widely seen as having the leading role in the military aspects of U.S. policy toward the region.

In consequence, there may be a danger of overlooking the role of the U.S. Army in a properly coordinated joint approach to the challenges of the Western Pacific. The U.S. Army role, however, is an essential component in the mix. For all its push to the sea, China at the moment remains essentially a continental power; China's strategic culture reflects long periods in which its main security preoccupations were with the defense, and sometimes the extension of, its territorial borders. This goes for most other countries in the region as well. Seven of the world's 10 biggest armies are to be found in Asia, and 21 of the 27 Asia-

Pacific nations traditionally have the Chief of Army as their Chief of Defense.[95] Many countries in the region, moreover, still suffer from major problems of domestic insurgency and are therefore required to engage in long, costly, and difficult land-force-centric campaigns to secure national integrity. In such a situation, an engagement approach that neglects the land dimension is unlikely to succeed. Accordingly, the U.S. Army Pacific Command (USARPAC) seeks to maintain "persistent engagement, forward presence, trained, and ready forces and an agile mission command" in order to cope with a wide range of theater contingencies.[96] Accordingly, all three services will need to contribute to the deterrence of China's assertiveness to its reassurance and to a strategy of wider engagement in the region.

Deterrence and the Military.

Despite the fact that "preventing and deterring future conflict relies on finding the right theater force posture" and that "winning the nation's wars has and will always be the U.S. Army's most essential mission,"[97] it is hard to conceive of a situation in which it would be necessary or even credible for the United States to engage in a direct land war with China. This does not, however, apply to the Korean Peninsula, where the explicit deterrence of North Korean aggression remains in many ways USARPAC's core mission in the Asia-Pacific theater. But this deterrence is not aimed at China and indeed is partly designed to avoid provoking it. With this significant exception, the U.S. Navy, Marines, and Air Force, rather than the Army, would be at the daily cutting edge of U.S. military deterrence of Chinese aggression, should that ever seem likely to occur.

Nonetheless, it is the Army's contention that the Air-Sea Battle construct, to the extent that it is a consciously deterrent strategy, "requires a joint force . . . You can't achieve in my opinion, A2AD with just air and sea . . . You have to look at it from a joint force perspective and not from a parochial perspective."

This was certainly the language of the Joint Operational Concept (JOAC) in November 2011. The Army should be able to provide the vital infrastructure, missile defenses, supply, and command-and-control facilities, even if not apparently in the forefront of any such Pacific-based campaign.[98] Some, indeed, advocate a shift in Army thinking away from mechanized maneuver and toward missile forces designed to deter through the capacity to defend allies and "hinder adversaries from projecting power themselves." Working with the U.S. Navy and Air Force, the Army's deployment of anti-ship missiles on land sites, it is argued, would "limit China's ability to inflict damage off the Asian mainland" and offer enhanced prospects for a blockade of Chinese shipping (or Offshore Control).[99] Others, though, defend the continued need for mechanized armor.[100]

However this maneuver/firepower debate works out, as an editorial in *DefenseNews* remarked: "There are few crowded battle-fields, and fewer theatres in which some land component will not be necessary to shape events or attain decisive results."[101] This is consistent with the official language, which talks of "integrated operations across all five domains," the need to maintain the capacity to "defend and respond in each warfighting domain" in order to ensure "the U.S. and allied expeditionary warfare model of power projection and maneuver."[102]

Contextual realities reinforce the point about the indispensability of a significant role for the Army in a recessed strategy of deterrence in the Western Pacific, not the least because of the very poor record since World War II of predictions about when and where the large-scale commitment of ground forces might prove to be necessary. To cope with unexpected contingencies, "we should be organized and prepared for a rapid response of widely dispersed expeditionary forces that converge to any crisis."[103]

The presence of U.S. forces in the region, moreover, is a matter of choice, not geography, since the area is far removed from the continental United States. There is then a significant **discretionary** element to the U.S. guarantee of less fortunately placed allies and partners such as Japan and South Korea. Accordingly, a policy of sea-based offshore-balancing (which implicitly retains the option of sailing/flying away if/when the going gets tough) needs to be sustained by a substantial presence ashore for maximum credibility and strategic effectiveness. Finally, the maintenance of a heavy land capability ashore in Korea with "(h)igh states of readiness and training for the North Korean threat that is the best deterrence to prevent it from actually occurring" requires the maintenance of demanding warfighting standards and helps provide ". . . the Army that everybody wants to be associated with."[104]

Moreover, the substantial buildup of Chinese naval/air capability, its relative lack of transparency, and the apparent furthering of its counterintervention strategy could certainly all be seen as a challenge to the U.S. maritime supremacy in the area. Up to now, the U.S. Navy had become accustomed to thinking of itself as the dominant naval player in the Western

Pacific, in fact if not theory, conceding China's pre-eminence in the continental theater. Now China appears to be seeking to transform this military balance to its own advantage. One probable consequence may be the unraveling of the standard maritime off-shore balancing narrative, which argues:

> ... that America can best contain our adversaries not by confronting them on land, but by maintaining our naval and air power and strengthening those smaller nations that see us as a natural counterweight to their larger neighbors.[105]

The more maritime China becomes, the less likely in some respects will all this seem possible.

Nonetheless, there is a substantial maritime component to the strategic tension between China and the United States. One of the most obvious signs is the defense of what the United States sees as freedom of navigation in waters the Chinese regard as their own. This has become one of the main irritants in the current relationship between the two countries, and, with the Chinese announcement of a new ADIZ in the East China Sea in November 2013, could easily get both more complicated and more dangerous operationally.[106] China maintains that unauthorized foreign air/naval activity in its economic exclusion zone (EEZ), including what the British call "military data gathering," is a kind of tactical/battlefield preparation, and so prejudicial to the security of China.[107] This activity, China claims, is a contravention of the UN Conference on Laws of the Sea (UNCLOS) Article 301, which requires parties to refrain from threatening the sovereignty of any state when exercising their rights in someone else's EEZ. The opening of the PLAN's new submarine base at Sanya, with its all important access to deep water, will no doubt have strengthened such perceptions. Should China be slowly developing a bastion approach for the deployment of its future submarine submersible ballistic missile (SSBNs), as the Soviet Union did in the Barents Sea and the Sea of Okhotsk, sensitivity to such data gathering would no doubt increase still further.[108] The *Impeccable* incident, after all, took place a mere 75 nautical miles southeast of the Sanya Naval Base.[109] The intensity and frequency of such U.S. activities is held to be evidence of Cold War thinking and a stumbling block to better military-to-military relations. The United States would regard all this as an instance of China seeking to change the rules rather than observe them. The same observation may be made about the USS *Cowpens* incident of November 26, 2013.

Further, China's conception of its EEZ and its near seas is that it is an abundant source of fish, oil, and gas resources essential to the national economy, an area of indisputable sovereignty that must be protected, a large defensive moat against unwelcome intruders, and a point of access to the wider ocean. For all these reasons, in Beijing's view, these are waters in which China's interests and expectations should be paramount. The unexpectedly harsh tone of China's response to the projected but canceled presence of the U.S. carrier *George Washington* in an exercise with the Republic of Korea's navy in the Yellow Sea after the sinking of the *Cheonan* (and by subsequent editorials in the *Global Times,* the English-language version of the official *People's Daily*), illustrates the point. The latter said:

> China undoubtedly needs to build a highly credible anti-carrier capacity. . . . Not only does China need an

39

anti-ship ballistic missile, but also other carrier-killing measures . . . Since US aircraft carrier battle groups in the Pacific constitute deterrence against China's strategic interests, China has to possess the capacity to counterbalance.[110]

China seems often to see itself as potentially encircled by foreign forces in local seas. Accordingly, Chinese commentators regularly and publicly condemn the forward presence of U.S. naval warships, and no longer accept — if they ever did — arguments that it has a stabilizing function that also works to the benefit of China. Thus, People's Liberation Army (PLA) Major General Luo Yuan declared: "The so-called forward presence means that the United States can send its gunboats to every corner of the world . . . This way, the United States can even claim the Yellow Sea and the South China Sea is covered within its security boundary."[111] Chinese commentators also point out that were the USS *George Washington* to have sailed into the Yellow Sea, its aircraft would have been capable of reaching Beijing. If we add to this a strategic culture deeply affected by the country's historic exposure to threats from the sea, not the least of which is in this particular area, and to the disastrous consequences for China of the failure to deter these activities, Chinese sensitivity to the unauthorized presence and activity in Chinese waters is understandable.

It is this context that China has seemingly embarked on a campaign of developing counterintervention capabilities that would put American forces at risk, should they enter the near seas in a manner to which China takes exception. The resultant anti-access/area denial (A2/AD) strategy,[112] as this has been dubbed by its prospective victims, appears to be a complex system-based sea denial strategy that makes use of sophisticated and resilient command, control, communications, computers, and intelligence, surveillance, and reconnaissance (C4ISR) facilities to detect and target hostile surface ships and to threaten them with a range of ballistic and cruise anti-ship missiles, delivered from land bases, land-based aircraft, submarines, and medium and small surface combatants. All of this strategy, it would seem, is accompanied by a cyber offensive intended to undermine the U.S. Navy and Air Force's electronic capacities to defend themselves and to sustain offensive operations. The United States seems to have been surprised by how rapidly key components of this strategy, such as the anti-satellite capacity revealed in 2009, the initial operating capacity of the DF-21D anti-ship ballistic missile in late-2010, and the J-20 fifth generation fighter that appeared in March 2011, have emerged. How effective all this would be militarily remains an issue of considerable debate, but even its critics accept that A2/AD puts U.S. forward presence in the near seas at significantly greater hazard, and thus may serve the Chinese political/deterrent purpose of such a strategy.

The effect is reinforced by what seems to be a reasonably concerted political and legal campaign to demonstrate to the other countries of the region that U.S. naval intentions, especially, but not exclusively, in the EEZ, are provocative, destabilizing, and illegal in terms of the UNCLOS (which, as they rarely fail to point out, the United States has so far not ratified). This combination of threatened hard power and deployed soft power has had its effect on Asia opinion, and certainly is not conducive to improved relationships between the two main actors in this drama.[113] It is not inconceivable that this combined power could lead to a serious while unintended incident at sea, or, indeed, in the air above it, at least equivalent to the collision of American and Chinese aircraft near Hainan in 2001.

Since the foundation of the Republic, the United States, for its part, has always felt that it has no choice but to defend the principle of freedom of navigation in what it regards as the Global Commons, if necessary, against the strongest of powers.[114] For Washington, this was and remains a point of high principle. In January 1918, accordingly, President Woodrow Wilson made "Absolute freedom of navigation upon seas outside territorial waters" the second of his Fourteen Points.[115]

More recently, the U.S. Navy tends to think of the world ocean in global rather than regional terms, as the world's greatest maneuver space, and is acutely sensitive to the way in which a precedent established in one area could well be applied elsewhere. Hence, the conduct of freedom of navigation exercises "with attitude" in the past, such as the Gulf of Sirte cruises of the mid-1980s and the bumping incident involving the USS *Caron* and a Soviet warship in the Black Sea in 1988.[116] In the Asia-Pacific theater, the sheer size of the Pacific Ocean (and the time it takes to cross even portions of it) requires open access to, and forward presence in, the Western Pacific for the United States to service its alliances and protect its interests. Without this forward presence, the current security system could unravel, and local powers could be forced to seek unwelcome accommodations with their great neighbor in a manner that would also be against U.S. national interests. An avoidance of such a situation has contributed to the interest of the U.S. Navy and Air Force in developing the concept of Air-Sea Battle mentioned earlier.

The atmospherics have undoubtedly been worsened by the way that the Air-Sea Battle was seen to be not an operational concept — an exercise in coordination between naval and air forces against the development of sea denial capabilities around the world[117] — but instead as a **strategy** specifically aimed at China.

Nonetheless, there is a reasonable chance that in time with the low-key maintenance of their positions on warships and the EEZ (which seems usually to be current practice[118]), the tensions over this point between China and the United States can be managed without irreparable damage to the prospect of their entering into a closer relationship, while still retaining this cardinal point of strategic interest and legal principle for the United States. Chinese officials have now publicly admitted[119] that they too have conducted military surveillance operations in other people's EEZs, specifically around Hawaii and Guam, and so may be following the example set by the Soviet Union in earlier days in which they first resisted, then adopted, Western conceptions of the freedom of the seas during UNCLOS negotiations.[120] In this instance, a fairly low-key military action in defense of the principle of free navigation (the USNS *Impeccable*, after all, is civilian manned and not a standard warship, and neither were the vessels harassing it) appears to have achieved both aims.

Some authorities have suggested an alternative deterrent posture for the United States, which retains the notion of coercive pressure on China but accepts the argument that military-technological and legal problems make it increasingly difficult to do so via a forward presence and Air-Sea Battle. Conceding the Western Pacific as a mutually denied battlespace, the notion of Offshore Control instead aims to discipline

Chinese behavior by threatening pressure on its sea lines of communication at some distance away from the Chinese mainland. Capitalizing on China's manifest nervousness about what President Hu once called its Malacca Dilemma difficulties, this strategy may seem somewhat less provocative to Beijing, as it would not call for a substantial American naval/air presence in China's near seas. This alternative strategy, however, has its practical, legal, and technological difficulties, too, and its greater effectiveness as a deterrent to China and as a reassurance to Japan and South Korea is by no means accepted by all. The outcome of this arcane debate only seems likely to be settled by greater clarity about the future technological feasibility of the U.S. Navy and Air Force's capacity to maintain a decisive presence in the Western Pacific.[121] But this, of course, is a debate about the **means** of U.S. deterrence of China, not its necessity or aim.

The long-term strategic effectiveness of such a deterrent would partly also depend on how it is communicated to China and indeed to the rest of Asia. In keeping with the notions of recessed deterrence discussed earlier, a low-key approach would seem likely to work the best.

Reassurance and the Military.

China's admission that it, too, gathers intelligence in the EEZs of other countries suggests that a degree of maritime convergence between the United States and China may be expected despite their current rivalries. The two countries certainly have increasing interests in common. China has as much at stake in the safe transition of the 74,000 or so merchant vessels that ply the Straits of Malacca and the pass through the South

China Sea every year as any other major player in the global system. Recent events have shown that China, moreover, is as vulnerable as any other country—and maybe more than most—to the illicit activities of the Iranian Revolutionary Guard in the Gulf, the depredations of Somali pirates, and, indeed, to disorder and instability ashore. As an increasingly maritime power with extensive state interests and a growing diaspora, China seems likely to have an increasing interest in the Freedom of Navigation, the world ocean as a flow resource, and the general defense of the sea-based trading system. This explains Chinese participation in the international counterpiracy effort off Somalia and its slow integration with Western efforts.[122] Equally, there is a clear attempt to normalize relations between the two navies.[123]

This is entirely consistent with the aims of the U.S. Navy's recent doctrinal statement, *A Cooperative Strategy for 21st Century Seapower*. The establishment of a global maritime partnership designed to protect the good order at sea and the safe and timely sailing of the world's merchant shipping on which the world's peace and prosperity rest means that navies and coast guards need to cooperate against anything that threatens maritime security, whether that takes the form of piracy and other forms of maritime crime, direct attack by forces hostile to the system, or the incidental effects of inter- and intrastate conflict. With aims that seem identical, the Chinese would seem to be a natural and increasingly important component in a Mahanian community of commercial interests and righteous ideals in what might be envisaged as more of a shared kind of maritime dominance aimed not at state but at, in the main, nonstate threats—exercised by a rather different set of navies than Mahan had in mind.

Nonetheless, frictions remain, as does the possibility of unwanted incidents at sea — hence, the ongoing bilateral talks about the prevention of unintended incidents at sea routinely held between the United States and Chinese navies. So far, progress in these has been slow, even glacial. The Chinese are apt to represent their attendance at the talks as a withdrawable concession to the American side, rather than as an acceptance that the resolution of these difficulties would be in their own interest. Where the United States wishes to talk tactics — identifing dangerous behaviors at sea that should be avoided by agreement — the Chinese focus on matters of high principle. Because these incidents commonly take place in what China regards as its near-seas, these discussions usually then get bogged down in the absence of agreement about who owns what and what jurisdiction the owner is entitled to have. But the essential point is that mutual understanding is advanced by these talks, even if no substantial formal agreement seems possible in the forseeable future. In the meantime, the low-key way in which both sides have preserved their principles without major incident since March 2009, suggests that the normal maritime rules of the road and such systems as the Code for Unexpected Encounters at Sea (CUES) can be used instead as a workaround, if not a solution.[124]

In November 2012, China's Defense Minister, General Liang Guangli, argued: "We should develop the ties between us, between our two militaries, touch on some of our differences, resolve conflicting views . . . our two countries' ties are very important."[125] The future relationship of the two countries, the need to cooperate over Korean security, and the threat of violent extremist organizations were among the issues of common interest to be explored. This idea was pushed further in a meeting between Secretary of Defense Chuck Hagel and Liang's successor, General Chang Wanquan, in August 2013.[126] There is a substantial land component to this, since these broader purposes need to be served at least as much by armies talking together as navies and arguably much more, given the particular influence of the dominating PLA. The two armies do interact bilaterally, thereby increasing mutual understanding, even a degree of trust. Such bilateral interactions are intended to influence the thought processes and strategic assumptions of the PLA's future leaders and indeed to develop the capacity for low-level interoperability slowly in such areas as humanitarian assistance—areas in which the land component has a particularly important role to play. For such interoperability, exercises are key.[127]

Accordingly, the U.S. Army Corps of Engineers regularly participates in the annual Yangxi Forums and through such means advances the capacity for functional cooperation in disaster management such as logistics and the provision of medical services.[128] The Chinese appear to be impressed by the extent to which USARPAC can operate multilaterally in this kind of activity and are probably increasingly aware of the gaps in their own responses and the greater need to think through the second- and third-order consequences of their actions—or sometimes lack of them. These low-key and functional initiatives are reinforced by a variety of two-way exchanges such as band visits, military student interchanges,[129] and mid-level officer exchanges. These trust building exercises may be slow in their effect and consequence, but it is important to recall the significance of the fact that there was little activity of this sort between the United

States and previous potential power challengers such as Nazi Germany, Imperial Japan, or the Soviet Union.

This degree of slow professional military convergence is unlikely to produce fast and decisive results and is certainly not without its difficulties. This approach faces innumerable problems, such as finding the necessary funding and the fact that the United States tends to give its officers higher levels of operational responsibility than people of other ranks in foreign services (which makes matching sensitive and difficult). Much worse, though, is the fact that some elements in the Chinese military and party hierarchy remain deeply suspicious of this kind of bilateral exchange and regard it as a covert means of U.S. infiltration into the Chinese military system, threatening the party's control of the Army.[130] Explicit and highly charged suggestions that Chinese personnel are being groomed for this purpose by the U.S. military are hardly likely to encourage Chinese participants in such exchanges to "open up." At the same time, the Chinese may well be very unwilling to let their own deficiencies be known by others.

Nor is U.S. participation in such exchanges untrammeled. All USARPAC proposals of this kind have to be specifically approved to ensure that they do not break the legal constraints of the National Defense Authorizations Act 2000, in such areas as the export of military technology and the sensitivity of military equipment to be used. Media exposure can cause difficulties as well, if it identifies the involvement of controversial Chinese personnel, for example. Finally, each proposal has to gain institutional approval through the United States Pacific Command (USPACOM) and be put in the budget. None of this is as byzantine as the equivalent Chinese process. But it also illustrates the effect of the absence of trust and the need to build it up if the United States and China are to develop as security partners.

One important aspect of military-to-military trust building would be the encouragement of still further transparency in the Chinese defense decisionmaking process. This remains a contentious issue — with the amount, trajectory, and consequences of Chinese defense spending being fiercely contested by both sides.[131] Nonetheless, tentative moves toward enhanced transparency are under way,[132] and can be facilitated through regular personal contacts, exercises, and institutional initiatives such as the establishment of a regular strategic and economic security dialogue. All of this helps stabilize and normalize the relationship between the two countries.[133]

That said, the task of crafting a general policy that constructively combines the twin strategic requirements of reassurance and deterrence may prove especially hard when it is confronted with specific and practical issues. One of these is Taiwan, given the inexorably widening gap between Taipei's capacities to defend itself and China's growing might. As Ambassador Freeman has observed:

> We are coming to a point at which we can no longer finesse our differences over Taiwan. We must either resolve them or live with the increasingly adverse consequences of our failure to do so.[134]

An American policy of calculated ambiguity — of limited military help to Taiwan and restraint on Taipei, alongside constant reminders to Beijing of the adverse consequences of assertive action, even if militarily successful — is still the distinguishing characteristic of American policy. These constant reminders might well be thought to include the provision of "air defense and other key capabilities to allies and friends in the event of a Taiwan contingency."[135]

Fortunately, the Taiwan issue appears to have much less salience than once it did, given the level of practical **rapprochement** between Taipei and Beijing. Sadly, precisely the same tensions and contradictions for the United States can be seen in the ongoing maritime jurisdictional disputes over the South and East China Seas, most especially between Japan and China. Here, as remarked earlier, the United States seeks to balance its strategic aim of securing a constructive relationship with China against the urgent tactical requirement to support its allies while not facilitating their adventurism.

Wider Engagement and the Military.

The current U.S. drive to engage-and-partner in the Asia-Pacific appears to have two objectives. The first of these is to engage with partners able to assist in the deterrence/reassurance of China, usually through their own independent channels and subjects of communication with Beijing, but sometimes through the provision of facilities of one sort or another that support a forward U.S. presence (such as Australia, Japan, South Korea, and Singapore). The second objective is to facilitate the management or resolution of local problems that could disturb local stability and threaten interests commonly held around the region and which, in some cases, might otherwise exacerbate relations between Beijing and Washington. The U.S. Army's presence in South Korea is a good example. Partly, it acts as a deterrent on North Korean aggression, and partly, it may serve as a means of mediating the troubled relations between South Korea and Japan, thereby contributing to a stability that is in the interests of both Beijing and Washington.[136]

The key requirement for both objectives is to avoid creating the impression in Beijing that the United States is weaving a web of countries around China's strategic periphery that is intended to contain its rise. This impression would not be acceptable to the great majority of regional countries. Their sheer diversity of character and interest would in any case make this impossible, and provides a practical restraint on the United States and a source of relief and even acceptance to China.[137]

The Global Maritime Partnership (GMP) construct in CS21, for example, was generally welcomed in the region as it was around the world. It demonstrates tacit acceptance of a leading security role for the U.S. Navy and the fact that, for the moment at least, in Kishore Mahbubani's words:

> The real reason why most international waterways remain safe and open – and thereby facilitate the huge explosion of global trade we have seen—is that the American Navy acts as the guarantor of last resort to keep them open. Without the global presence of the U.S. Navy, our world order would be less orderly.[138]

GMP serves both purposes, since it addresses common problems, such as the threat of piracy, drug smuggling, international terrorism, human trafficking, and catastrophic natural disasters, such as extreme weather. Any of these could directly threaten sea-based trade and other legitimate forms of sea-use and indirectly threaten the local stability afloat and ashore upon which that trade depends. That is the reason for the multitude of cooperative naval operations designed to curb these activities, and to build up local capacities to handle them in the future and, where necessary, to engage in security sector reform. These activities include bilateral exercises such as the Cooperation Afloat Readiness and Training (CARAT) exercises held between the U.S. Navy and nine Southeast and South Asia navies, and multilateral naval exercises like the Rim of the Pacific (RIMPAC), which help develop the necessary capabilities. Exercise engagement will also tend to be supported by port visits; military-to-military contacts; and the provision of security assistance in the shape of platforms, equipment, and skills training. The transfer of two ex-U.S. Coast Guard cutters to the Philippines is a recent example.

This action, however, does raise the issue of China's perception of such activities. The conduct of naval engagement with allies and partners can be seen as potentially hostile by third parties. If this is not, as in this case, the intention, the handling of such engagements needs to be conducted with finesse. Fortunately, local partners will usually be only too pleased to help the United States do so.

The land equivalent of such engagement is at least as important in the Asia-Pacific Region where, as already remarked, the human terrain is dominated by the army.[139] The USARPAC co-hosted Pacific Army Chiefs Conferences, to which most of the region's Army chiefs come, has the highest visibility. Below that come a host of regional Army get-togethers to address cooperation in such issues as: the contribution of military medicine to common health threats (not the least of which is pandemic disease); de-mining (a major issue in much of Southeast Asia, Myanmar, and Sri Lanka); counterterrorism training (Special Forces); action against police brutality, and corruption; and, disaster management so necessary in the Asia-Pacific Region.

The U.S. Army's hard-won experience in counter-insurgency and security force assistance from General Douglas MacArthur's experience in the Philippines in the 1930s and in Japan from 1945 to 1950, through the former Yugoslavia, Colombia, Liberia, Iraq, and Afghanistan, retains clear relevance in an area where many countries continue to face real internal security problems, including, of course, China.[140] The success of the Joint Special Operations Task Force-Philippines is a case in point.[141]

Armies, like navies, are what some call an epistemic community. Because of their shared experience and outlooks, they often talk better to each other than they do to their own civilians and diplomats, first about the narrow functional issues of the day and then, as confidence and a degree of trust build, about wider security concerns.

As another means of facilitating its strategy of wider engagement, the Army is progressing its system through which units align with certain areas to become more familiar with their culture, language, and requirements, together with an expansion of its International Military and Educational Training (IMET) programs (such as happened with Indonesia, Malaysia, Cambodia, the Philippines, and Thailand). Toward this purpose, the Army's Foreign Area Officers program has particular utility in that it produces means by which local expertise can be fed into the American decisionmaking system, and assistance can be provided to local countries on a whole variety of civilian-military issues of particular value to those countries transitioning into democracies. Although the extent of this program's utility should not be exaggerated, it represents something of a shift away from straight warfighting toward the more consciously calibrated and restrained employment of military power.[142]

To a large extent, these "engage-and-partner" exercises are focused on managing what some call nontraditional (but no less important) security threats, which, by their nature and effect, are commonly regarded as security threats throughout the region. Constructively, defending good order against nontraditional threats in this way is not only usually in the direct national interest of the United States, but it also helps head off local instabilities that potentially could exacerbate relations between it and China.

A still-more-ambitious variant of the policy is the encouragement of the development within the region of net security exporters rather than consumers. This is accomplished by engaging with countries that have "expressed their intentions to expand their regional influence to use their influence to assume a greater share of future regional security responsibilities,"[143] perhaps so they can develop the capacity to lead, deploy, and participate in peacekeeping or humanitarian operations. This may develop into attempts to build up relations with allies and partners like Korea, Japan, India, and Australia, as part of U.S. policy of trying to identify and prioritize regional leaders.[144] Each of these states is an independent actor with its own agendas, constraints, and priorities, both in the region and globally. None of them (with the possible exception of Japan under Prime Minister Shinzo Abe) would wish to be seen as part of an international coalition designed to contain China. All of them seem interested in maintaining and expanding their capacity to ensure security and stability in the Asia-Pacific, to "deter aggression, coercion, or provocative actions by potential spoilers,"[145] and to help prevent and respond to crises. For these reasons, this kind of engagement tends to focus on the development of higher-end skills such as preparing for expeditionary operations.

The long, slow, cautious buildup of a defense relationship with India is probably the best recent example. In January 2012, the U.S. Department of Defense, (DoD) Defense Strategic Guidance, stated that:

> The United States is also investing in a long-term partnership with India to support its ability to serve as a regional economic anchor and provider of security in the broader Indian Ocean region.[146]

The process for this partnership is through the sale of high-profile military equipment like the C-17 and C-130J transport aircraft and the P-8 maritime patrol aircraft. India became the second largest defense buyer from the United States in 2011. More than 50 bilateral exercises took place with India in 2011, which included a variety of maritime security, counterterrorism, salvage, and diving exercises, plus those dealing with unexploded ordnance. The Indians have observed RIMPAC and hold MALABAR exercises involving the United States and India. Participation in MALABAR has been expanded in some years to include Japan, Australia, and/or Singapore. The annual MALABAR is considered the premier annual bilateral maritime exercise.[147] At the same time, India is the subject of USARPAC's largest bilateral exercise series, part of which is intended to help India develop more expeditionary skills, a more ambitious leadership role, and the capacity to handle contingencies. There is enough confluence of national interest for the U.S. military to help in this way.

Nonetheless, there are considerable constraints on the process. Partly, these reflect bureaucratic, political, and institutional constraints within India, and partly because India is another Asia-Pacific country that values its independence of decision; it has a long cultural-strategic tradition of marching to the beat of its own drum, and it intends to continue to do so. This is true, more or less, of all of Washington's other security partners in the region, so any prospect of an engage-and-partner initiative ending up as an Asia-Pacific version of the North Atlantic Treaty Organization (NATO) is exceedingly remote. Still less likely for the same reason is the prospect of this initiative becoming an anti-Chinese coalition, compounded in most cases by the very high and increasing levels of mutually beneficial trade that individual countries do with China. Hence, Chinese complaints about this prospect are episodic and seem to have a distinctly formulaic quality. From this point of view, the more Beijing is involved and feels able to participate in these engagement exercises, the better — hence its likely involvement in RIMPAC 2014 is to be welcomed.

The prevailing and sometimes inconvenient independence of view characteristic of the region would seem to reinforce the notion that the U.S. policy of engage-and-partner is most likely to lead to an increasingly multipolar Asia-Pacific. This should serve as the basis of an enduring security partnership between China and the United States better than either a largely bilateral relationship of two Asia-Pacific giants surrounded by small fry on the one hand, or of China versus the rest of Asia on the other.

CONCLUSION AND RECOMMENDATIONS

Several broad conclusions about the tricky course to be followed would seem to emerge from this review. The first is that it would be unwise of the United States to seek to establish a quasi-coalition of any sort, since this would be regionally unpopular and would feed Beijing's paranoia. The second is that the United States may need to exercise caution in its involvement in disputes between China and other players in the region. Both in the Scarborough Shoal/Second Thomas Reef dispute between China and the Philippines, and the Senkaku/Daioyu Islands dispute between China and Japan, there is the danger that incautious support for local partners could encourage local adventurism and risk the broader objective of securing an enduring and beneficial security relationship with China.[148]

The risk of such adventurism reinforces the need for U.S. restraint, lest its broader strategic objectives in the Asia-Pacific become much harder to achieve. But at the same time, most analysts would agree that Chinese assertiveness over such issues and any ambitions that some in Beijing may have about re-establishing the habits of deference from others throughout the region need to be prevented. The Finlandization of Asia would be a profoundly destabilizing development that needs to be deterred. The United States therefore must steer a complex course between deterrence and reassurance in its relationship with a rising China. In such a tricky and holistic policy involving the full spectrum of hard, sticky, and soft power, the U.S. military in the region is likely to have crucial roles to play in both dimensions of this policy and in a supporting campaign of wider engagement.

Summary and Recommendations.

- Despite its long strategic history, world power is a relatively new concept for China. Mistakes, insensitivities, and ambiguities must be expected and, when not deterred, responded to sensitively.

- This will require the United States to maintain and display substantial joint forces in the Asia-Pacific region, alongside its active soft and sticky power engagement.
- To serve the overall purpose of securing a new, sustainable, and mutually beneficial relationship with China, U.S. deterrent policies will need to be recessed, implicit rather than overtly confrontational — unless particular Chinese *demarches* require a robust response.
- For the same reason, Washington will need to reassure Beijing and to demonstrate that its peaceful rise is regarded as a needed first step in developing a new relationship between the two countries.
- A descent into bilateralism in the Asia-Pacific (whether the result of a policy of Chinese Finlandization of the region or the U.S. orchestration of a quasi-coalition against China) would be profoundly destabilizing and unwelcome to most countries in the region. The varied agenda of a multiplicity of second-tier actors is an effective constraint on Chinese adventurism.
- Accordingly, the engage-and-partner strategy of U.S. forces in the Asia-Pacific region should aim to improve military-to-military relations with China while contributing to the capacity of other countries in the region to work with China as independent, confident, and effective actors in their own right.
- This engage-and-partner strategy should focus on responses to such apparently lower-order threats as international terrorism, transnational crime ashore and afloat, and humanitarian disasters, because these could easily prove desta-

bilizing regionally while offering good prospects of cooperation with a new and relatively more powerful China.

ENDNOTES

1. Dana H. Allin and Erik Jones, *Weary Policeman: American Power in an Age of Austerity*, London, UK: Routledge for the International Institute for Strategic Studies (IISS), 2012, p. 170.

2. Niall Ferguson, "The Decade the World Tilted East," *The Straits Times*, January 7, 2010.

3. Minxin Pei, "Think Again: Asia's Rise," *Foreign Policy*, June 22, 2009, p. 5.

4. See Arthur Cotterell, *Western Power in Asia: Its Slow Rise and Swift Fall, 1415-1999*, Singapore: John Wiley & Sons, Asia, Pte. Ltd, 2010; and Ian Morris, *Why the West Rules — For Now*, London, UK: Profile Books, 2011.

5. Thus, the conclusion of the influential Kishore Mahbubani, *The New Asian Hemisphere: The Irresistible Shift of Global Power to the East*, New York, Public Affairs, 2008.

6. The internal Chinese debate about what Beijing's official "Harmonious World" foreign policy after the era of U.S. primacy actually means can be seen through a comparison between Professor Zhao Tingyang's *The Tianxia System*, 2005, and Senior Colonel Liu Mingfu's *The China Dream*, 2010. *The Tianxia System* uses traditional Chinese ideas to craft a new world order, while *The China Dream* argues that the PRC needs to have a military rise to guard its economic rise. These two books are important because they became social phenomena and media events that put their authors into the spotlight. They provoked debates that spread their influence far beyond their core audiences of scholars and military officers into China's broader civil society. The possibilities discussed range from a more modest pursuit of world harmony, to the more active project of harmonizing the world — by force, if necessary. See William A. Callahan, *China: The Pessoptimist Nation*, Oxford, UK: Oxford University Press, 2010.

7. "Remarks to the Australian Parliament," Washington, DC: The White House, Office of the Press Secretary, November 17, 2011.

8. *Sustaining U.S. Global Leadership: Priorities for the 21st Century,* Washington, DC: U.S. Department of Defense (DoD), January 2012, pp. 1-3; *The National Military Strategy of the United States of America: Redefining America's Military Leadership,* Washington, DC: DoD, 2011, pp. 10-11.

9. Vice-President Joseph Biden, quoted in Mark Landler, "Biden Tries to Soothe Asia Tension," *The International New York Times,* December 7-8, 2013.

10. *China Daily,* December 2012.

11. Kor Kian Beng, "China's Leaders Fly the Extra Mile to Push Foreign Policy," *The Straits Times,* November 11, 2013.

12. Zhou Wa, "Western Views of China Increasingly Positive," *China Daily,* May 14, 2012.

13. Chin-Hao Huang, *China's Soft Power in East Asia: A Quest for Status and Influence?* Special Report #42, Washington, DC: National Bureau of Asian Research, January 2013.

14. "US Lacks World's Trust, Poll Finds," *The Guardian,* September 12, 2012; see "America's Global Image Remains More Positive than China's," Washington, DC: Pew Research Center, July 18, 2013; and Jeremy Au Yong, "More think US losing standing abroad," *The Straits Times,* December 5, 2013.

15. Rowan Callick, "Asian 'Pivot' Losing its Edge," *The Australian,* October 8, 2013; Cameron Stewart, "US Failing to Back Its Asia Pivot," *The Australian,* October 9, 2013; Alan Dupont, "Pivot to Asia Has Not Fallen Off Its Axis," *The Australian,* October 15, 2013.

16. Nirmal Ghosh, "Anti-China Sentiment a Challenge for Myanmar," *The Straits Times,* January 14, 2013; Drew Hinshaw and Chuin-Wei Yap, "China Tensions Stoked by Ghana Arrests,"

The Wall Street Journal, June 10, 2013. The United Nations World Tourism Organization figures showed that at a collective $102 billion in 2012, Chinese tourists are now the biggest tourist spenders. But this may be a problem: Ho Ai Li, "China's Loud and Loutish Travellers," *The Straits Times*, June 3, 2013.

17. "Chinese Military Makes Anti-US Movie," *The Straits Times*, November 3, 2013, from *The New York Times*; Wang Gungwu, "Xi'an Challenge Counters the Shanghai Syndrome," *The Straits Times*, November 11, 2013.

18. Despite all the statistics concerning rising anger about corruption, unfair land acquisition practices, and pollution, successive and reputable public opinion surveys in China continue to show a population that is broadly content with the way things are going, especially when measured by the key evidence of expectations that the lives of their children will be better than theirs. The Chinese system has shown itself to be a good deal more enduring than some expected 15 years ago.

19. Yuan Guiren, "Promote Mutual Understanding," *China Daily*, November 21, 2013.

20. World Bank Development Indicators, 2008, available from *siteresources.worldbank.org/DATASTATISTICS/Resources/WDI08 supplement1216.pdf*. See also Rajiv Biswa, *Future Asia*, London, UK: Palgrave, 2013.

21. "China's Trade Figures Bounce Back from Crisis," *The Straits Times*, January 11, 2010.

22. Niall Ferguson, *The Ascent of Money: A Financial History of the World*, London, UK: Penguin Books, 2009, p. 285.

23. Unpublished presentation paper at East Asia Institute, Singapore, February 26, 2010. For evidence of Chinese perceptions of this, see Meng Jing, "Cleared For Take-Off," *China Daily*, December 5, 2012; Wang Chuo, "Going the Extra Yard," and Professor Yu Hongyuan, "A Revolution Is Here and Clean Energy Is the Spark," both from *China Daily*, December 28, 2012.

24. See statement of Norman R. Augustine, Retired Chairman and CEO of the Lockheed Martin Corporation, before the Democratic Steering and Policy Committee, Washington, DC, U.S. House of Representatives, January 7, 2009.

25. Josef Joffe, *The Myth of America's Decline*, New York: Liveright, 2013.

26. Hence its pursuit of free trade deals with Southeast Asia and advocacy of a Regional Comprehensive Economic Partnership (RCEP), Editorial, *The Straits Times,* October 30, 2013.

27. Some have sought to do so, however. Ruchir Sharma, "China's Illusory Growth Numbers," *The Wall Street Journal*, November 1, 2013; a balanced view is taken by Timothy Beardson, *Stumbling Giant: The Threats to China's Future*, New Haven, CT: Yale University Press, 2013.

28. "For China, Spending Is Less Easy Than it Looks," *The Wall Street Journal*, February 14, 2013.

29. These may be assessed through successive articles in *The Wall Street Journal,* including Timothy Beardson, "Don't Count on China to Bail Out the US," February 14, 2013; Ruchir Sharma, "China Has its Own Debt Bomb," February 27, 2013; "Tensions Mount as China Grabs Farms for Homes," February 15, 2013. Also see Jonathan Walton, *Intensifying Contradictions: Chinese Policing Enters the 21st Century*," Washington, DC: National Bureau of Asian Research, February 2013, available from *nbr.org/publications/element.aspx?id=647.*

30. J. Stapleton Roy (Ex-US Diplomat), "Drift Toward Strategic Rivalry," Paper for East-West Center, February 20, 2013.

31. Wen Jiabao, quoted in Chris Buckley and Zhou, "China GDP Target Cut Helps Fight External Pressures: Wen," *Reuters,* March 14, 2012.

32. Ambassador Charles W. Freeman, Jr., "Beijing, Washington, and the Shifting Balance of Prestige," Remarks to China Maritime Studies Institute, U.S. Naval War College, Newport, RI, May 10, 2011; Presentation of Paul Haenle of the Carnegie-Tsinghua Center for Global Policy, Beijing, China, November 2013.

33. Christopher A. McNally, "How Emerging Forms of Capitalism are Changing the Global Economic Order," *Asia-Pacific Issues*, No 107, Honolulu, HI: East-West Center, February 2013. Though the fact that the RMB has appreciated by some 40 percent since 2005 largely removes one cause of frequent U.S. complaints.

34. James Dobbins, quoting a RAND study, "War With China," *Survival*, August-September 2012, p 8.

35. Sam Tangredi, *Futures of War: Towards a Consensus View of the Future Security Environment*, Newport, RI: Alidade Press, 2008, pp 105-107; Andrew S. Erickson and David D. Yang, "Using the Land to Control the Sea: Chinese Analysts Consider the Antiship Ballistic Missile," and Eric Hagt and Mathew Durnin, "China's Antiship Ballistic Missile: Developments and Missing Links," both in *Naval War College Review*, Autumn 2009, pp. 53-86 and 87-116, respectively.

36. Robert O. Work, *The US Navy: Charting a Course for Tomorrow's Fleet*, Washington, DC: Center for Strategic and Budgetary Assessments (CSBA), 2008, p. 71. See also remarks by Dr. Donald C. Winter, Secretary of the Navy, at the Sea Air Space Exposition, Washington, DC, April 3, 2007.

37. Cited in Michael Richardson, "Looming Defence Cuts Threaten Global Security," *The Straits Times*, February 18, 2013.

38. *Global Times*, October 29, 2013.

39. Peh Shing Huei, "Hu Defends Track, Calls for War on Graft," *The Straits Times*, November 9, 2012.

40. *Ibid.*; Mr. Xi cited in George Galdorisi, "The United States Pivot to the Pacific," *Asia Pacific Defence Reporter*, October 2013.

41. James Holmes, "China's Maritime Strategy Is More than Naval Strategy," China Brief 8, Washington, DC: Jamestown Foundation, April 2011.

42. With, however, the substantial exceptions of the Tang, middle-Song and late-Ming dynasty periods. But the first of these was more commercial and maritime than naval; the second also was more riverine and coastal than open-sea. The third, while totally remarkable in its level of technological and operational ambition, was something of an unsustainable "flash in the pan." See Louis Levathes, *When China Ruled the Seas,* Oxford, UK: Oxford University Press, 1994.

43. Wendell Minnick, "Report Shows Rapid Rise of China's Defense Industry, Russia's Role," *Defense News,* December 10, 2012.

44. Joint Operational Access Concept (JOAC), Version 1.0, November 22, 2011.

45. For a vigorous statement of this, see Work, *The US Navy: Charting a Course for Tomorrow's Fleet.* This broadly is also the conclusion of the U.S. Government's intelligence review, *Global Trends 2030,* and Andrew Erickson and Adam Liff, "A Player, but no Superpower," available from *ForeignPolicy.com.* But for a countervailing view of the need and possibility of just such a development, see Colonel Liu Mingfu, lately of the National Defence University in Beijing, *The China Dream,* Beijing, China: Zhonguo, 2010.

46. Martin Jacques, *When China Rules the World,* New York: Penguin, 2009, pp. 409-413; Yasheng Huang, *Capitalism with Chinese Characteristics,* New York: Cambridge University Press, 2008.

47. "Get Used to Beijing's Rising Power: Chinese Paper," *The Straits Times,* December 8, 2012.

48. For such dangers in power transition, see Steve Chan, "Exploring Puzzles in Power-Transition Theory: Implications for Sino-American Relations," *Security Studies,* Vol. 13, No. 3, pp. 103-141.

49. Niall Ferguson, "The Trillion Dollar Question," *The Guardian,* June 2, 2009; "China Should Aim to be World No 1," *The Straits Times,* March 2, 2010. This article discusses the recent book, *The China Dream,* by Colonel Liu Mingfu of China's National Defence University. See also Zhang Min, *Chinese Are Not Afraid:*

New Threats to Chinese Defense Security and China's Response Strategies, Shanghai: People's Publishing House, 2013. It is only fair to remark that the United States has its hawks too. See Kai Liao, "The Pentagon and the Pivot," *Survival*, Vol. 55, No. 3, June-July 2013, pp. 95-114.

50. Henry Kissinger, Address at the 8th IISS Global Strategic Review Conference, Geneva, Switzerland, September 10-12, 2010, quoted in "A World Full of Fault lines," *The Straits Times*, December 7, 2010.

51. Yuka Hayashi and Jeremy Page, "US, Japan Warn China in Island Row," *The Wall Street Journal*, November 25, 2013.

52. Dilip Haro, "A New Fluidity to Power Plays," *The Straits Times*, February 26, 2010.

53. "Anti-China Rhetoric in US 'a Mistake'," *The Straits Times*, February 9, 2012.

54. This policy might be characterized as being somewhere between the conditional offense/defense and defensive balancing options outlined in Michael D. Swaine *et al.*, *China's Military and the US-Japan Alliance in 2030*, Washington, DC: Carnegie Endowment for International Peace, 2013 — more deterrent than the latter, less than the former.

55. These were especially evident in the naval field. See Stephen Roskill, *Naval Policy between the Wars: the Period of Anglo-American Antagonism, 1919-1929*, London, UK: Collins, 1968, especially pp. 204-233, 300-330, 433-466. For the ruthless U.S. attack on British economic interests, see Lawrence James, *Churchill and Empire: Portrait of an Imperialist*, London, UK: Weidenfeld and Nicolson, 2013, pp. 323-328.

56. Qiao Xonsheng, "A World to Win and Little to Lose," *China Daily*, February 21, 2011.

57. U.S. Deputy Defense Secretary Ashton B. Carter, Remarks at the Woodrow Wilson Center, Washington, DC, October 3, 2013.

58. These principles are discussed in Carlyle A. Thayer, "China-US Defence Ministers Meet: Not Quite a New Type of Great Power Relationship," *Thayer Consultancy Background Brief,* August 14, 2013.

59. This is essentially the argument of Hugh White, *The China Choice: Why America Should Share Power*, Collingwood, Ontario, Canada: Black, Inc., 2012. See Denny Roy's review of this work in *Survival*, Vol. 55, No. 3, June-July 2013, pp. 183-202.

60. See Robert Lieber, *Power and Willpower in the American Future: Why the United States is not Destined to Decline*, Cambridge, UK: Cambridge University Press, 2012; and responses to it by Christopher Layne, Paul Macdonald, Joshua Shrifson, and others, available from *H-DIPLO@H-Net.MSU.edu*, July 2013.

61. Freeman, p. 4.

62. Layne, Footnote 51.

63. Henry Kissinger, *On China*, London, UK: Allen Lane, 2011, p. 348. For other illustrations of the requirement to take China's distinctive strategic culture into account when providing it with behavioral incentives and disincentives, see also pp. 218, 237, 376, 270, 394, 407, 450, 462, 506, 515.

64. Kissinger, *On China*, p. 237.

65. Hua Liming, "China Has a Role to Play in Mideast," *China Daily*, January 8, 2013; International Crisis Group, *China's Central Asia Problem*, Asia Report No. 244, February 27, 2013.

66. Yong Deng, *China's Struggle for Status*, Cambridge, UK: Cambridge University Press, 2008. See Ching Cheong, China dealing with security threats within and outside," *The Straits Times*, November 21, 2013.

67. Rory Medcalf, "China Throws Away a Chance to Lead," *The Wall Street Journal*, November 15-17, 2013.

68. David C. Kang, *China Rising: Peace, Power and Order in East Asia*, New York: Columbia University Press, 2007; Denny Roy,

"More Security for Rising China, Less for Others?" *Asia Pacific Issues*, No. 106, Honolulu, HI: East-West Center, 2013.

69. Lai-han Chan, "China's Vision of Global Governance: A New World Order in the Making or Old Wine in a New Bottle?" Draft paper for RSIS Conference on China's Role in Global and Regional Governance, Singapore, March 2011.

70. Anthony Reid and Zheng Yangwen, eds., *Negotiating Asymmetry: China's Place in Asia*, Singapore: NUS Press, 2009.

71. Article "PRC's 'New Diplomacy' Stress on 'More Active' International Role," July 11, 2005, quoted Chin-Hao Huang, *China's Soft Power in East Asia: A Quest for Status and Influence?* Special Report #42, Washington, DC: National Bureau of Asian Research, January 2013.

72. This may also underlie China's creation for the first time of a National Security Commission, *ibid.*; and Kor Kian Beng, "New CCP Policies Raise Questions for Region," *The Straits Times*, November 23, 2013.

73. John Bolton, "How to Answer China's Muscle-Flexing," *The Wall Street Journal*, December 6, 2013.

74. I am grateful to my colleague, Dr. Hoo Tiang Boon, for his insights in this area.

75. Kissinger, *On China*, pp. 173, 217. Kissinger maintains that this is a development of the Sun Tzu notion of "combative coexistence," a characteristic much evidenced by Chinese behavior in crises over the offshore islands.

76. Carlos Tejada, "China Lashes Back at Hacking Claims," *The Wall Street Journal*, February 20, 2013; "China Hackers Breached US, Aussie Security: Report," *The Straits Times*, May 19, 2013.

77. Dana H. Allin and Erik Jones, *Weary Policeman: American Power in an Age of Austerity*, London, UK: Routledge for IISS, 2012, pp. 167-168, 200-201.

78. The domestic and political costs of these levels of defense spending, on the other hand, are more difficult to calculate and may prove significantly less easy to bear.

79. Eberhard Sandschneider, "Is China's Military Modernization a Concern for the EU?" in Zaborowski, pp. 40-41; Mahbub-nai, 2008, p. 105.

80. Tangredi, p. 103.

81. Jeremy Au Yong, "US Seeks to Balance Asia Goals, China Ties," *The Straits Times*, December 7, 2013; Mark Landler, "Biden Tries to Soothe Asia Tension," *The International New York Times*, December 7-8, 2013.

82. Richard Fontaine, "Asians Hedge against China," *The Wall Street Journal*, December 6, 2013. Thus the ADIZ initiated in November had the unwelcome effect for Beijing of drawing together South Korea and Japan, two countries with a testy relationship in recent times.

83. Quoted in Denny Roy.

84. Discussions with Chinese scholars at the Council for Security Cooperation in the Asia-Pacific preparatory meeting, Singapore, December 2012.

85. Niall Ferguson and Moritz Schularick, "The US and China Both Need Economic Rehab," *The Wall Street Journal*, November 7, 2013.

86. Chin-Hao Huang, *China's Soft Power in East Asia: A Quest for Status and Influence?* Special Report #42, Washington, DC: National Bureau of Asian Research, January 2013.

87. Quoted Michael Richardson, "Securing Allies Amid China's Rise," *The Straits Times*, February 2, 2013.

88. Zhang Jie and Li Zhifei, "Security Challenge in 2013," *China Daily*, January 10, 2013; Cheong Suk-Wai, "US Moves 'to Cooperate with, Not Contain, China'," *The Straits Times*, December 6, 2012.

89. Robert Ross, quoted in William Cheong, "US Should Focus on Easing China's Anxieties," *The Straits Times*, January 14, 2013.

90. Cheong Suk-wai; David Kang, "Balancing US, China Interests in East Asia," *The Straits Times*, October 24, 2012.

91. Xi Jinping, quoted in "Putin, China's Xi Vow 'Strategic' Support in First Meeting," AFP Staff Writers, Moscow, Russia, March 23, 2010.

92. Brahma Chellaney, "Averting Power Disequilibrium in Asia," *The Straits Times*, November 15, 2012; see also "Pacific Is Big Enough for All of Us: Clinton," *The Straits Times*, November 16, 2012.

93. Fareed Zakaria, *The Post American World and the Rise of the Rest*, London, UK: Penguin, 2009, pp. 254-279; Timothy Garton Ash, "Only a Strategic Partnership with China Will Keep This New Dawn Bright," *The Guardian*, November 27, 2008.

94. Hillary Clinton, "America's Pacific Century," *Foreign Policy*, November 2011.

95. "Partnering in the Pacific Theater: Assuring Security and Stability through Strong Army Partnerships," United States Army, Pacific, October 1, 2012, p. 2.

96. *Ibid.*, p. 1.

97. *Ibid.*, p. 11.

98. Sydney J. Freedberg, Jr., "Army Creates 'Strategic Landpower' Office with SOCOM, Marines: Odierno Defends Budget," *Aol Defense*, November 1, 2012: JOAC Version 1.0, November 22, 2011.

99. Jim Thomas, "Why the U.S. Army Needs Missiles," *Foreign Affairs*, May-June, 2013, pp. 137-144; Terence K. Kelly *et al.*, *Employing Land-Based Anti-Ship Missiles in the Western Pacific*, Santa Monica, CA: RAND, 2013.

100. Chris McKinney, Mark Elfendahl, H. R. McMaster, "Why the U.S. Army Needs Armour," *Foreign Affairs,* May-June, 2013, pp. 129-136.

101. "Rest, Renew & Rethink," *Defense News,* October 22, 2012.

102. "Air-Sea Battle: Service Collaboration to Address Anti-Access and Area Denial Challenges," Washington, DC: Air-Sea Battle Office: Department of Defense, May 2013, pp. I, 2, 4. See also Richard A. Bitzinger and Michael Raska, "The AirSea battle Debate and the Future of Conflict in East Asia," *RSIS Policy Brief,* February 2013; and Elbridge Colby, "Don't Sweat AirSea Battle," *The National Interest,* July 31, 2013, available from *nationalinterest. org/print/commentary/dont-sweat-airsea-battle-8804.*

103. Lieutenant General (Ret.) Duane Thiessen, USMC, in Joel Wuthrow *et al., The US Army in Asia: Opportunities and Challenges,* Washington, DC: Center for Naval Analyses, August 2013, p. 10.

104. Wuthrow, p. 10.

105. Peter Beinart, quoted in Dana H. Allin and Erik Jones, *Weary Policeman: American Power in An Age of Austerity,* London, UK: Routledge for IISS, 2012, p. 88.

106. Michael Auslin, "China's Regional Aggression Takes Flight," *The Wall Street Journal,* November 26, 2013.

107. Ren Xiaofeng and Cheng Xizhong, "A Chinese Perspective," *Marine Policy,* Vol. 29, No. 2, 2005, pp. 139-146.

108. Tetsuo Kotani, "What China Wants South China Sea," *The Diplomat,* July 18, 2011.

109. Oriana Skylar Mastro, "Signalling and Military Provocation in Chinese National Security Strategy," *Journal of Strategic Studies,* April 2011, pp. 219-244, especially p. 220; Mark Valencia, "The Impeccable Incident: Truth and Consequences," *China Security,* Spring 2009.

110. Staff Writers AFP Beijing, September 7, 2010; "China Needs 'Carrier-Killer Missile: Press'," citing *Global Times,* Sep-

tember 6, 2010. This was unexpected, since China did not protest against the presence of the *George Washington* in the Yellow Sea in 2009.

111. Luyo Yuan, "PLA General: US Engaging in Gunboat Diplomacy," *People's Daily*, August 12, 2010, cited in Manicom.

112. This, of course, is an American term, not a Chinese one.

113. The problem for the United States is compounded by the fact that, for their own reasons, other countries in the region, including India, Malaysia, Thailand, and Vietnam, adopt not-dis-similar policies toward the EEZ, although in their case, China is probably the main target.

114. Hence, the so-called Quasi War with France, 1798-1800, and the War with Britain in 1812.

115. R. Cranston, *The Story of Woodrow Wilson*, New York: Simon & Schuster, 1945.

116. This latter was resolved by a U.S.-Soviet agreement signed September 23, 1989, at Jackson Hole, Wyoming, in which the Soviets agreed on the right of foreign warships to transit territorial waters on "innocent passage." In return, the United States undertook not to engage in more of such freedom-of-navigation exercises. At issue in this case were foreign rights in the territorial sea, not the EEZ.

117. As it was in the UK.

118. Discussions with USPACOM and PACFLT, May 2013. The USS *Cowpens* incident of November 26, 2013, however, shows the fragility of this assumption. See Carl Thayer, "US Cowpens Incident Reveals Strategic Mistrust Between U.S. and China," *The Diplomat*, December 17, 2013.

119. At the Shangri-La Dialogue, Singapore, May 2013. See IISS Report, August 2013; Rory Medcalf, "Is China 'Reciprocating' US Maritime Surveillance?" Sydney, Australia: Lowy Institute for International Policy, *The Interpreter*, June 1, 2013. Additionally, some Chinese analysts are now making the point that there may be significant distinctions in the frequency and intensity of such

military data gathering, with some types of (macro and strategic) intelligence being somewhat less objectionable than more immediately provocative (battlefield) activity.

120. James Kraska, *Maritime Power and the Law of the Sea*, Oxford, UK: Oxford University Press, 2011, pp. 31, 106-107.

121. See TX Hammes, "Offshore Control: A Proposed Strategy for an Unlikely Conflict," Washington, DC: National Defense University, Strategic Forum, July 2012. Also see Sea Mirski, "Stranglehold: The Context, Conduct and Consequences of an American Naval Blockade of China," and E. B. Montgomery, "Reconsidering a Naval Blockade of China: A Response to Mirski," *Journal of Strategic Studies*, Vol. 36, No. 3, May 4, 2013, pp. 385-421, 616-623. The feasibility and desirability of a forward U.S. presence is the distinguishing difference between the two Carnegie alternative options.

122. The Chinese now participate in intelligence-sharing arrangements in Bahrain, and rescue internationally flagged merchant vessels, not just their own.

123. Grace Jean, "USN Conducts Gulf of Aden Counter-Piracy Training with PLAN," *Jane's Defence Weekly*, September 4, 2013; and "Chinese Warships Pull into Pearl Harbor for US Port Visit," *Jane's Defence Weekly*, September 18, 2013.

124. Discussions with USPACFLT staff. See also David Griffiths, *U.S.-China Maritime Confidence Building: Paradigms, Precedents, and Prospects*, Newport, RI: U.S. Naval War College, China Maritime Studies Institute, 2010.

125. Quoted in "China Tries to Allay Fears Over Its Military Build-Up," *The Straits Times*, November 28, 2012, a point echoed in "US Calls for Closer Military Ties with China," *The Straits Times*, May 29, 2013.

126. Daniel Wasserbly, "US, Chinese Officials Seek to Bolster Defence Relationship," *Jane's Defence Weekly*, August 28, 2013.

127. "US China Militaries Hold Disaster Relief Exercise," *The Straits Times*, December 1, 2012.

128. USARPAC Discussions, March 2013.

129. West Point cadets regularly do one of their semesters in China, for example.

130. "Chinese Military Makes Anti-US Movie," *The New York Times*, reproduced in *The Sunday Times*, Singapore, November 3, 2013.

131. Compare, for example, Zhu Zhe and Zhang Haizhou, "Defense Spending Lower Despite Risks," *China Daily*, March 9-15, 2012; and Jeremy Page, "China to Lift Spending on Defense," *The Wall Street Journal*, March 5, 2012.

132. Wu Jiao and Mo Jingxi, "Spokesmen System to Boost Military Transparency," *China Daily*, November 21, 2013; Wen Ya, "First Military Spokespeople," *Global Times*, November 22, 2013.

133. Tao Wenzhao, "Unprecedented Endeavour," *China Daily*, May 9, 2012.

134. Freeman, Remarks, p. 6; see also Elbridge Colby, "Can We Save Taiwan?" *The National Interest*, October 18, 2013, available from *nationalinterest.org/commentary/can-we-save-taiwan-9257*; and "Alarm Over the Taiwan Strait," *The Wall Street Journal*, November 7, 2013.

135. Comments by Major General (Ret.) John Landry in Wuthrow, p. 7.

136. Jonathan Eyal, "The US: Bridge Over Troubled Waters," *The Straits Times*, November 4, 2013.

137. "US Rebalance: Potential and Limits in Southeast Asia," *IISS Strategic Comments*, December 19, 2012.

138. Kishore Mahbubani, *The New Asian Hemisphere: The Irresistible Shift of Global Power to the East*, New York, NY: Public Affairs, 2008, p. 105.

139. Daniel Wasserbly, "Army Chief Outlines Ground Force Role in New Strategy," *Jane's Defence Weekly*, January 27, 2013.

140. Paul McLeary, "As US Army Looks to Asia, Partners Are Critical," *Defense News,* October 22, 2012; Vago Muradian, "Odierno Pushes BCT Revamp, Must-have Programs," *Defense News,* November 5, 2012; Michelle Tan, "YS Army Boosting Budget, Doing More in Pacific," *Defense News,* December 10, 2012; Cheng Cheong.

141. Wuthrow, p. 7.

142. Jeremy Au Yong, "US to Boost Defence Drills with Asian," *The Straits Times,* November 17, 2012; Wuthrow, pp. 1, 6, 11.

143. "Partnering in the Pacific Theater," p. 7.

144. Derek S. Everson, "When Foreign Policy Goals Exceed Military Capacity, Call the Pentagon," Washington, DC: Foreign Policy Research Institute, February 2013.

145. "Partnering in the Pacific Theater," p. 7.

146. *Sustaining U.S. Global Leadership: Priorities for 21st Century Defense*, Washington, DC: U.S. Department of Defense, January 5, 2012, p. 2.

147. Report to Congress on U.S.-India Security Cooperation, Washington, DC: U.S. Department of Defense, November 2011, p. 3.

148. Li Ying, "US Not Ready to be Philippines' Savior over Huangyan Island," *China Daily,* May 21, 2012; Simon Tisdall, "Militarism or Reform? As the Sabres Rattle, Japanese PM Must Decide," *The Guardian,* December 17, 2013.